JavaScript Handbook

JavaScript Design Patterns

JavaScript Patterns Unlocked: Module, Singleton, Factory, and More

By Laurence Lars Svekis

Dedicated to

Alexis and Sebastian

Thank you for your support

For more content and to learn more, visit

https://basescripts.com/

JavaScript Handbook

JavaScript Design Patterns

Summary

The **JavaScript Handbook: Design Patterns** offers a comprehensive, hands-on approach to learning the most essential design patterns for modern JavaScript development. Covering foundational patterns like **Module, Singleton, Factory, Observer, and Prototype**, this book provides everything you need to build clean, maintainable, and scalable applications.

Each pattern is explained in detail, starting with clear definitions and followed by hands-on coding exercises, real-world examples, and multiple-choice quizzes. These interactive elements enable readers to **apply their knowledge immediately**, ensuring a deeper understanding of each concept.

Key Takeaways:

- **Learn the most essential design patterns** to streamline your development process.

- **Practice with real-world coding exercises** that simulate practical development scenarios.
- **Test your understanding** with multiple-choice quizzes and step-by-step solutions.

This book is designed for **beginners and experienced developers alike**, providing a structured, interactive learning experience. By the end, readers will have the knowledge and skills to **recognize coding problems, apply the correct design pattern, and write clean, efficient code**.

Introduction

Welcome to the **JavaScript Handbook: Design Patterns**—your guide to mastering one of the most critical aspects of JavaScript development. This book is designed to help developers, from beginners to experienced programmers, understand and apply essential design patterns to build clean, maintainable, and scalable applications.

Design patterns offer proven solutions to common coding challenges, making your development process more efficient and your code more reliable. Through practical examples, interactive exercises, and multiple-choice quizzes, this book demystifies complex concepts like the **Module, Singleton, Factory, Observer, and Prototype patterns**, among others. Each pattern is broken down with clear explanations and hands-on coding examples, allowing you to **understand how, when,**

and why to use each pattern. With this knowledge, you'll be able to recognize coding problems, identify the appropriate pattern, and confidently apply it to real-world projects. Whether you're preparing for a technical interview or seeking to become a more proficient JavaScript developer, this book will equip you with a toolkit of design patterns that will streamline your workflow and make you a more versatile coder.

Introduction to the Module Pattern in JavaScript

What is the Module Pattern?

The module pattern is a design pattern used in JavaScript to encapsulate private and public data and methods. Before the advent of modern JavaScript module systems (like ES Modules or CommonJS), developers often used the module pattern to create self-contained units of code that kept internal details private while exposing a public API.

Why Use the Module Pattern?

1.   **Encapsulation of Code**: It helps you group related variables, functions, and functionality into a single unit.
2.   **Preventing Global Pollution**: The module pattern keeps variables and functions out of the global namespace, preventing naming collisions and promoting cleaner code.

3.   **Data Privacy**: By leveraging closures, you can create private variables and methods that cannot be accessed from the outside.

4.   **Public API Exposure**: It provides a controlled way to expose certain parts of the code to the outside world (the "public" methods) while keeping other parts hidden ("private" details).

How Does It Work?

The module pattern typically uses an Immediately Invoked Function Expression (IIFE). An IIFE is a function that runs immediately after it is defined. The structure looks like this:

```
var myModule = (function() {
    // Private variables and functions
    var privateVar = "I am private";
    function privateMethod() {
        console.log("This is a private
method!");
    }


    // Public methods and variables
```

```
        return {
            publicVar: "I am public",
            publicMethod: function() {
                console.log("This is a public
method!");
                console.log("Accessing privateVar
inside: " + privateVar);
                privateMethod();
            }
        };
    })();
```

In the snippet above, `myModule` holds the returned object, which contains `publicVar` and `publicMethod`. The variables and functions defined inside the IIFE but not returned remain private and inaccessible from the outside.

Key Concepts

IIFE (Immediately Invoked Function Expression):
An IIFE looks like this:

```
(function() {
    // code
})();
```

1.   The parentheses around the function definition ensure it's treated as an expression, and the trailing ( ) executes it immediately.

2.   **Closures**:

The module pattern relies on closures. Variables defined in an outer function remain accessible to inner functions even after the outer function finishes execution. In the module pattern, the IIFE returns an object that can still access private data through closures, thus "closing over" the local variables.

3.   **Private vs. Public Members**:

o   **Private**: Declared inside the IIFE but not returned.

o   **Public**: Exposed as part of the returned object.

Benefits

•   **Maintainability**: Code is easier to read, maintain, and reuse.

•   **Security**: Private data is less prone to accidental modifications.

•   **Namespace Management**: Reduces global variable usage and prevents naming conflicts.

Drawbacks

•   **Testing Private Members**: Private functions and variables can be harder to test directly since they are hidden.

- **Refactoring Complexity**: Breaking the code into multiple smaller modules may become cumbersome if you rely too heavily on a single large module.

Detailed Code Examples

Example 1: Simple Counter Module

```
var counterModule = (function() {
    var count = 0; // private variable


    function increment() {
        count++;
    }


    function decrement() {
        count--;
    }
```

```javascript
    return {
        getCount: function() {
            return count;
        },
        increase: function() {
            increment();
            console.log("Count after increment:
" + count);
        },
        decrease: function() {
            decrement();
            console.log("Count after decrement:
" + count);
        }
    };
})();


// Usage
counterModule.increase(); // Count after
increment: 1
counterModule.increase(); // Count after
increment: 2
```

```
counterModule.decrease(); // Count after
decrement: 1
console.log(counterModule.getCount()); // 1
// console.log(count); // Error: count is not
defined globally
```

Example 2: Revealing Module Pattern

The "Revealing Module Pattern" is a variant that explicitly maps private members to public pointers, making it clearer which members are exposed.

```
var calculatorModule = (function() {
    var total = 0; // private
    function add(num) {
        total += num;
    }
    function subtract(num) {
        total -= num;
    }
    function reset() {
        total = 0;
    }
```

```
    function getTotal() {
        return total;
    }


    // Reveal only the methods we want to make
public
    return {
        add: add,
        subtract: subtract,
        reset: reset,
        getTotal: getTotal
    };
})();


calculatorModule.add(10);
calculatorModule.subtract(3);
console.log(calculatorModule.getTotal()); // 7
calculatorModule.reset();
console.log(calculatorModule.getTotal()); // 0
```

Example 3: Namespaced Modules

You can create multiple modules under a single namespace:

```javascript
var app = app || {};


app.moduleA = (function() {
    var privateMessage = "Hello from module A";
    return {
        greet: function() {
            console.log(privateMessage);
        }
    };
})();


app.moduleB = (function() {
    var privateValue = 42;
    return {
        getValue: function() {
            return privateValue;
        }
    };
```

```
})();
```

```
app.moduleA.greet(); // Hello from module A
console.log(app.moduleB.getValue()); // 42
```

Multiple-Choice Questions

1.   Which best describes the Module Pattern in JavaScript?

A. A pattern used to handle asynchronous code execution.

B. A design pattern for organizing code into reusable classes.

C. A pattern using closures and IIFEs to create private and public members.

D. A pattern that removes the need for objects entirely.

Answer: C.

The module pattern relies on IIFEs and closures to encapsulate variables and functions, resulting in private and public members.

2.   What does IIFE stand for?

A. Immediately Invoked Function Expression

B. Internal Invoked Functional Execution

C. Important Invoked Function Executor

D. Immediately Integrated Function Expansion

Answer: A.

IIFE stands for Immediately Invoked Function Expression.

3.   **Which of the following is a characteristic of an IIFE?**

A. It can never return a value.

B. It is executed immediately after it's defined.

C. It must always be anonymous.

D. It cannot contain private variables.

Answer: B.

An IIFE executes immediately as soon as it is defined.

4.   **In the module pattern, what is the purpose of returning an object from the IIFE?**

A. To export public methods and properties.

B. To ensure the function runs only once.

C. To allow recursion within the module.

D. To bind the module to the global window object.

Answer: A.

Returning an object exposes the public interface of the module.

5.   **What can be considered a major benefit of the module pattern?**

A. Global scope pollution.

B. Easily accessible private variables from outside.

C. Encapsulation and avoiding namespace collisions.

D. It prevents closures.

Answer: C.

The module pattern encapsulates code and avoids polluting the global scope.

6. **Which of these is NOT a disadvantage of the module pattern?**

A. Testing private members is harder.

B. Potential complexity in refactoring large modules.

C. Might require more memory usage than global variables.

D. It prevents any public methods from being created.

Answer: D.

The module pattern does allow public methods; that's the whole point of returning a public API.

In the following code, which is a private variable?

```
var myModule = (function() {
    var secret = "hidden";
    return {
        reveal: function() { return secret; }
    };
})();
```

7. A. myModule

B. secret

C. reveal

D. (function() { ... })

Answer: B.

secret is a private variable, accessible only inside the IIFE.

8. **Which of the following patterns is closely related to the module pattern and explicitly maps private members to public pointers?**

A. Singleton Pattern

B. Constructor Pattern

C. Revealing Module Pattern

D. Prototype Pattern

Answer: C.

The Revealing Module Pattern explicitly returns an object literal mapping private members to public keys.

9. **How do closures help in the module pattern?**

A. By preventing variables from being garbage collected.

B. By allowing inner functions to remember the environment in which they were created.

C. By making all variables global.

D. By preventing IIFEs from running automatically.

Answer: B.

Closures allow functions to retain access to their parent scope's variables, enabling private data.

10. **Which is true about the module pattern and global variables?**

A. It encourages the use of many global variables.

B. It completely eliminates global variables.

C. It reduces the need for global variables, but typically one global reference is made for the module.

D. It makes global variables automatically private.

Answer: C.

Usually, the module is assigned to a single global variable (e.g., `var myModule = ...`), reducing global namespace pollution.

11. **The module pattern is often used in older JS codebases because:**

A. Modern bundlers and ES modules weren't widely available in older environments.

B. The module pattern is newer than ES modules.

C. It is mandated by ECMAScript 6.

D. It doesn't rely on closures.

Answer: A.

Before ES Modules and bundlers became common, the module pattern was a popular way to create modular code.

12. **What happens if you do not return an object from the IIFE in the module pattern?**

A. You can't have private variables anymore.

B. You won't have a public interface to access.

C. The IIFE won't run.

D. An error is thrown at runtime.

Answer: B.

Without a returned object, no public methods or variables are exposed.

13. **Which keyword is not required to create a module pattern using IIFE?**

A. `function`

B. `return`

C. `var` or `const` to hold the module

D. `class`

Answer: D.

The module pattern does not require the `class` keyword.

Consider this code:

```
var moduleX = (function() {
    var count = 0;
    return {
        inc: function() { count++; },
        get: function() { return count; }
    }
})();
moduleX.inc();
console.log(moduleX.get());
```

14.   What is logged to the console?

A. `undefined`

B. `0`

C. 1

D. An error

Answer: C.

After one increment, `count` is 1, so

`console.log(moduleX.get())` prints 1.

15.   **What is a key reason to use the module pattern?**

A. To immediately globalize every variable in the script.

B. To manage and maintain code structure and data privacy.

C. To replace all functions with classes.

D. To ensure that variables persist across page reloads.

Answer: B.

The module pattern helps in organizing code and keeping data private.

16. **If you have a private function inside a module, how can you call it externally?**

A. Directly by its name.

B. By exposing it through the returned object.

C. By calling `window.privateFunctionName()`.

D. By converting it into an arrow function.

Answer: B.

To call it externally, you must expose it in the module's returned object.

17. **Which symbol pair typically wraps the IIFE function definition?**

A. {}

B. ()

C. []

D. <>

Answer: B.

IIFEs are wrapped in ( ) both around the function expression and at the end to invoke it.

18. **In the module pattern, what does the returned object represent?**

A. The private variables.

B. The public API of the module.

C. The entire global namespace.

D. Unused code.

Answer: B.

The returned object represents the public API that other code can use.

19. **The module pattern was heavily used before ES6 modules because:**

A. Browsers did not natively support module imports.

B. It was the only pattern that worked in ES6.

C. It is slower than ES modules.

D. It required TypeScript.

Answer: A.

Before ES6, browsers didn't support a native module system, so module pattern was a workaround.

20. **The IIFE in the module pattern is crucial because:**

A. It ensures that private variables are created anew every time the module is called.

B. It prevents any variables from being created.

C. It ensures immediate execution and creation of a closure.

D. It forces the use of this keyword.

Answer: C.

The IIFE ensures the module's code runs once and sets up closures to maintain private state.

10 Coding Exercises with Full Solutions and Explanations

Exercise 1: Basic Private and Public Methods

Task: Create a module `mathModule` that has a private variable `pi = 3.14159` and two public methods: `circumference(radius)` and `area(radius)`. `circumference(radius)` returns `2 * pi * radius`, and `area(radius)` returns `pi * radius * radius`.

Solution:

```
var mathModule = (function() {
    var pi = 3.14159;

    function circumference(r) {
        return 2 * pi * r;
    }

    function area(r) {
        return pi * r * r;
    }
```

```
    return {
        circumference: circumference,
        area: area
    };
})();
```

```
// Explanation:
// pi is private. circumference and area are
returned publicly, using pi internally.
console.log(mathModule.circumference(10)); //
62.8318
console.log(mathModule.area(10)); // 314.159
```

Exercise 2: Counter with Reset

Task: Create a module counter with a private variable count.
Expose three public methods: increment(), decrement(),
and current() that returns the current count. Also add a
reset() method to set count back to 0.
Solution:

```
var counter = (function() {
    var count = 0;
    function increment() { count++; }
    function decrement() { count--; }
    function reset() { count = 0; }
    function current() { return count; }


    return {
        increment: increment,
        decrement: decrement,
        reset: reset,
        current: current
    };
})();


counter.increment();
counter.increment();
console.log(counter.current()); // 2
counter.reset();
console.log(counter.current()); // 0
```

Explanation:

The `count` variable is private. We provide a public API to manipulate and read it.

Exercise 3: Module with Private Helper Function

Task: Create a module `stringModule` that has a private function `reverseString(str)` and a public function `isPalindrome(str)` that uses `reverseString` to determine if a string is a palindrome.
Solution:

```
var stringModule = (function() {
    function reverseString(str) {
        return
str.split('').reverse().join('');
    }
    function isPalindrome(str) {
        return str === reverseString(str);
    }
    return {
        isPalindrome: isPalindrome
    };
```

```
})();
```

```
console.log(stringModule.isPalindrome("level"))
; // true
console.log(stringModule.isPalindrome("house"))
; // false
```

Explanation:

reverseString is private and not accessible outside.
isPalindrome uses it internally.

Exercise 4: Config Module

Task: Create a configModule that stores private configuration
(like apiKey and apiUrl) and exposes methods
getApiKey() and getApiUrl() to retrieve them.
Solution:

```
var configModule = (function() {
    var apiKey = "12345-abcde";
    var apiUrl = "https://api.example.com";
```

```
function getApiKey() { return apiKey; }
function getApiUrl() { return apiUrl; }


return {
    getApiKey: getApiKey,
    getApiUrl: getApiUrl
};
})();


console.log(configModule.getApiKey()); //
"12345-abcde"
console.log(configModule.getApiUrl()); //
"https://api.example.com"
```

Explanation:

Sensitive data like apiKey and apiUrl remain private. Only getters are exposed.

Exercise 5: Todo List Module

Task: Create a `todoModule` that stores a private array of todos. Public methods: `add(todo)`, `remove(index)`, and `list()` that returns all todos.
Solution:

```
var todoModule = (function() {
    var todos = [];


    function add(todo) {
        todos.push(todo);
    }


    function remove(index) {
        if (index >= 0 && index < todos.length)
{
            todos.splice(index, 1);
        }
    }
```

```javascript
    function list() {
        return todos.slice(); // return a copy
    }


    return {
        add: add,
        remove: remove,
        list: list
    };
})();


todoModule.add("Learn JavaScript");
todoModule.add("Write Code");
console.log(todoModule.list()); // ["Learn
JavaScript", "Write Code"]
todoModule.remove(0);
console.log(todoModule.list()); // ["Write
Code"]
```

Explanation:

The `todos` array is not accessible externally, ensuring controlled manipulation.

Exercise 6: Bank Account Module

Task: Create a `bankAccount` module with a private `balance` variable. Public methods: `deposit(amount)`, `withdraw(amount)`, and `getBalance()`.
Solution:

```
var bankAccount = (function() {
    var balance = 0;


    function deposit(amount) {
        if (amount > 0) balance += amount;
    }


    function withdraw(amount) {
        if (amount > 0 && amount <= balance) {
            balance -= amount;
```

```
        }
    }


    function getBalance() {
        return balance;
    }


    return {
        deposit: deposit,
        withdraw: withdraw,
        getBalance: getBalance
    };
})();


bankAccount.deposit(100);
bankAccount.withdraw(30);
console.log(bankAccount.getBalance()); // 70
```

Explanation:

Balance remains private to prevent unauthorized changes directly.

Exercise 7: Settings Module with Default Values

Task: Create a module `settingsModule` that has private variables for `theme = "dark"` and `language = "en"`. Public methods: `setTheme(theme)`, `getTheme()`, `setLanguage(lang)`, and `getLanguage()`.

Solution:

```
var settingsModule = (function() {
    var theme = "dark";
    var language = "en";



    function setTheme(t) { theme = t; }
    function getTheme() { return theme; }
    function setLanguage(l) { language = l; }
    function getLanguage() { return language; }



    return {
```

```
        setTheme: setTheme,

        getTheme: getTheme,

        setLanguage: setLanguage,

        getLanguage: getLanguage
    };
})();


settingsModule.setTheme("light");
console.log(settingsModule.getTheme()); //
"light"
console.log(settingsModule.getLanguage()); //
"en"
```

Explanation:

The module encapsulates settings and provides controlled getters/setters.

Exercise 8: Memoization Module

Task: Create a fibModule that computes the nth Fibonacci number. Use a private cache object to store computed values. Public method: fib(n) that returns the nth Fibonacci number using memoization.

Solution:

```javascript
var fibModule = (function() {
    var cache = {};


    function fib(n) {
        if (n < 2) return n;
        if (cache[n]) return cache[n];
        cache[n] = fib(n - 1) + fib(n - 2);
        return cache[n];
    }


    return {
        fib: fib
    };
})();


console.log(fibModule.fib(10)); // 55
```

Explanation:

cache is private. Each computed Fibonacci number is stored, making subsequent calls faster.

Exercise 9: User Authentication Module

Task: Create authModule that stores a private isLoggedIn boolean and username. Public methods: login(user), logout(), and status() that returns the username if logged in, otherwise "Not logged in".

Solution:

```
var authModule = (function() {
    var isLoggedIn = false;
    var username = "";


    function login(user) {
        isLoggedIn = true;
        username = user;
    }


    function logout() {
        isLoggedIn = false;
```

```
            username = "";
    }


    function status() {
        return isLoggedIn ? "Logged in as " +
username : "Not logged in";
    }


    return {
        login: login,
        logout: logout,
        status: status
    };
})();


authModule.login("Alice");
console.log(authModule.status()); // "Logged in
as Alice"
authModule.logout();
```

```
console.log(authModule.status()); // "Not
logged in"
```

Explanation:

`isLoggedIn` and `username` are private, preventing external code from tampering directly.

Exercise 10: Timer Module

Task: Create a `timerModule` that has a private variable `startTime`. Public methods: `start()`, `stop()`, which returns the elapsed time in milliseconds, and `reset()` which resets the timer.

Solution:

```
var timerModule = (function() {
    var startTime = null;


    function start() {
        startTime = Date.now();
    }
```

```javascript
        function stop() {
            if (startTime === null) {
                return 0;
            }
            var elapsed = Date.now() - startTime;
            startTime = null;
            return elapsed;
        }


        function reset() {
            startTime = null;
        }


        return {
            start: start,
            stop: stop,
            reset: reset
        };
    })();
```

```javascript
timerModule.start();
setTimeout(function() {
    var elapsed = timerModule.stop();
    console.log("Elapsed time: " + elapsed + "
ms");
}, 500);
```

Explanation:

`startTime` is private, and the public methods handle timing operations securely.

Conclusion

The Module Pattern in JavaScript is a powerful, pre-ES6 approach to structuring code, promoting encapsulation, protecting the global namespace, and clearly separating public APIs from private implementation details. By understanding and practicing with the pattern, developers gain insight into closures, scoping, and code organization techniques that remain useful, even in the era of modern ES modules.

Introduction to the Singleton Pattern in JavaScript

What is the Singleton Pattern?

The Singleton pattern is a design pattern that ensures a class has only one instance, while providing a global point of access to that instance. In JavaScript, which is a prototype-based language rather than a classical OOP language, you don't have "classes" in the traditional sense (at least pre-ES6), but you can still implement singletons.

Why Use the Singleton Pattern?

1.   **Single Point of Access**: Having one and only one instance can be beneficial. For example, consider a configuration object or a database connection manager where multiple instances might cause conflicts.

2.   **Global State Management**: Singletons can be used to store global state in a controlled manner.

3.   **Resource Management**: Some resources, like caching objects or logging systems, might need a single consolidated instance.

41

Characteristics of the Singleton Pattern

1.   **Single Instance**: Only one instance of the object is created.

2.   **Lazy Initialization**: The instance is often created only when first requested.

3.   **Global Access Point**: The same instance is accessible throughout the codebase without the need to recreate it.

Implementing Singletons in JavaScript

Before ES6 modules and classes, singletons were often created using IIFEs or objects that store a single instance. In modern JavaScript, one can use classes and static methods or leverage closures.

Classic Singleton using Object Literals

```
var mySingleton = {
    property: "I'm the only instance!",
    method: function() {
        console.log("This method belongs to a
singleton instance.");
    }
};
```

```
mySingleton.method(); // "This method belongs
to a singleton instance."
```

While this approach creates a single instance, it doesn't
"enforce" a singleton since you could create another similar
object. However, mySingleton itself is just one object.

Singleton with Closure

```
var singleton = (function() {
    var instance; // private variable to hold
the instance


    function createInstance() {
        var obj = { name: "SingletonInstance",
timestamp: Date.now() };
        return obj;
    }
```

```
    return {
        getInstance: function() {
            if (!instance) {
                instance = createInstance();
            }
            return instance;
        }
    };
})();


var instance1 = singleton.getInstance();
var instance2 = singleton.getInstance();


console.log(instance1 === instance2); // true
```

Here, the singleton is an IIFE returning an object with a getInstance method. On the first call, it creates the instance. Subsequent calls return the same instance, ensuring only one instance exists.

ES6 Class-based Singleton

```
class Singleton {
    constructor() {
        if (Singleton.instance) {
            return Singleton.instance;
        }
        this.data = "Some data";
        Singleton.instance = this;
    }


    getData() {
        return this.data;
    }
}



const s1 = new Singleton();
const s2 = new Singleton();
console.log(s1 === s2); // true
```

In this ES6 class example, we store the instance as a static property `Singleton.instance`. Subsequent attempts to create a new instance return the previously created instance, preserving the singleton property.

Advantages of the Singleton Pattern

1.   **Controlled Access to a Single Instance**: Centralized management of certain resources or states.
2.   **Consistency**: Ensures that the global state remains consistent and not fragmented into multiple instances.
3.   **Configuration Management**: Useful when you have app-wide configuration or services that should be unified.

Disadvantages of the Singleton Pattern

1.   **Global State**: Singletons might encourage the use of global state, making the code harder to reason about.
2.   **Testing Difficulties**: Singletons can be harder to test because they maintain state across the entire application lifetime.
3.   **Tight Coupling**: Code that depends on singletons might be harder to refactor since multiple parts of the application rely on that single instance.

Multiple Code Examples

Example 1: Simple Singleton with an Object

```
var logger = {
    logs: [],
    log: function(message) {
        this.logs.push(message);
        console.log("Log added: " + message);
    }
};
```

```
logger.log("First log");
logger.log("Second log");
// logger is a single object used across the
codebase
```

Example 2: Singleton with Lazy Instantiation

```javascript
var dbConnection = (function() {
    var instance;
    function createConnection() {
        return {
            id: Math.random(),
            status: 'connected'
        };
    }
    return {
        getConnection: function() {
            if (!instance) {
                instance = createConnection();
            }
            return instance;
        }
    };
})();


var c1 = dbConnection.getConnection();
var c2 = dbConnection.getConnection();
console.log(c1.id === c2.id); // true
```

Example 3: Singleton in ES6 with a Symbol

```
const INSTANCE = Symbol('instance');


class Configuration {
    constructor() {
        if (Configuration[INSTANCE]) {
            return Configuration[INSTANCE];
        }
        this.config = { env: 'production',
version: '1.0.0' };
        Configuration[INSTANCE] = this;
    }


    get(key) {
        return this.config[key];
    }


    set(key, value) {
```

```
        this.config[key] = value;
    }
}


let config1 = new Configuration();
let config2 = new Configuration();
console.log(config1 === config2); // true
```

Multiple Choice Questions

1.   **What does the Singleton pattern ensure?**

A. Multiple instances of a class.

B. Only one instance of a class.

C. No instances of a class.

D. One instance per method.

Answer: B.

The Singleton pattern ensures only one instance is created.

2.   **How is a Singleton typically implemented in JavaScript?**

A. By creating a global variable for each instance.

B. By using closures or static properties to store a single instance.

C. By removing constructors from classes.

D. By using arrow functions only.

Answer: B.

Common approaches involve closures or class static properties to ensure a single instance.

3.   **Which is a benefit of the Singleton pattern?**

A. It guarantees an object has only one instance.

B. It allows multiple instances to be created easily.

C. It reduces the need for memory management.

D. It prohibits global state.

Answer: A.

The Singleton pattern ensures a single instance, which can be beneficial in certain scenarios.

4.   **Which of these is a downside of using a Singleton pattern?**

A. It simplifies testing.

B. It prevents global state.

C. It can make testing harder due to shared state.

D. It ensures multiple instances always exist.

Answer: C.

Since a singleton holds global state, it can complicate testing.

5.   **What is a common use-case for a Singleton?**

A. For every user-created object.

B. Database connections or configuration objects.

C. For array manipulation utilities.

D. For styling CSS dynamically.

Answer: B.

Singletons are often used for managing database connections, config objects, or loggers.

6. **In the classic JavaScript implementation using closures, how is the instance stored?**

A. As a global variable.

B. As a static property on the function.

C. In a local variable inside an IIFE (closure).

D. Inside the prototype property.

Answer: C.

The instance is often stored in a variable inside an IIFE, leveraging closures.

7. **Which pattern ensures that a class only has one instance and provides a global point of access to it?**

A. Factory Pattern

B. Singleton Pattern

C. Observer Pattern

D. Strategy Pattern

Answer: B.

The Singleton pattern is the correct choice.

8. **When the Singleton instance is created only when it is needed, this is known as:**

A. Early instantiation.

B. Forced instantiation.

C. Lazy instantiation.

D. Over instantiation.

Answer: C.

Creating the instance only upon the first request is lazy instantiation.

9.   Which keyword in ES6 can be used to define a class from which we can create a Singleton?

A. `class`

B. `function`

C. `var`

D. `singleton`

Answer: A.

The `class` keyword can be used to define classes in ES6, which can then be adapted for Singleton logic.

10.   In an ES6 Singleton, what prevents multiple instances from being created?

A. A conditional check in the constructor that returns an existing instance if present.

B. The `static` keyword alone.

C. Using `this` keyword only once.

D. The new keyword stops working.

Answer: A.

The constructor checks if an instance already exists and returns it if so.

11.   Which of the following is not necessarily true for a Singleton?

A. It must be implemented using a class.

B. It has only one instance.

C. It provides a global access point to that instance.

D. It may use lazy instantiation.

Answer: A.

Singletons can be implemented without classes (e.g., using closures or object literals).

12.   **What does "providing a global point of access" mean in the context of Singletons?**

A. The instance must be attached to the window object.

B. You have a single method or variable that returns the instance everywhere.

C. It can only be accessed from a global event.

D. It must be defined in the global scope.

Answer: B.

A global point of access means you have a known method or variable to get that single instance anywhere in the code.

13.   **If a Singleton object stores internal state, what is a potential problem?**

A. It reduces the size of the code.

B. The internal state might be changed by multiple parts of the code, causing unexpected issues.

C. It improves security.

D. It never leads to bugs.

Answer: B.

Shared state can be altered by various parts of the code, leading to unpredictable behavior.

14.   **In a testing environment, why can Singletons be problematic?**

A. They are always easy to mock.

B. They can't be accessed in tests.

C. They hold persistent state, making tests order-dependent and harder to isolate.

D. They automatically reset their state before each test.

Answer: C.

Persistent state in singletons can cause test interference and order-dependence.

15.   **Which pattern often leads to a global variable-like structure?**

A. Singleton Pattern

B. Adapter Pattern

C. Decorator Pattern

D. Module Pattern

Answer: A.

The Singleton can act like a globally accessible instance, similar to a global variable.

16.   **Can we create multiple Singletons in an application for different purposes?**

A. No, the term "Singleton" means only one singleton per application.

B. Yes, we can have multiple distinct singletons for different responsibilities.

C. Only if we use ES6 classes.

D. Only in Node.js.

Answer: B.

You can have multiple different singleton implementations, each ensuring a single instance of a particular kind of object.

17.   If you need to ensure only one instance of a logger object, how do you enforce it in JavaScript?

A. By using a closure or static property and returning the same instance every time.

B. By never calling the constructor.

C. By using `Object.freeze()`.

D. By throwing an error if the object is duplicated.

Answer: A.

You ensure a single instance by checking if an instance exists and returning it rather than creating a new one.

18.   Which is a sign that you might need a Singleton?

A. You find yourself creating the same object multiple times unnecessarily.

B. You want many copies of the same object.

C. You want to stop using global objects.

D. You do not want any state at all.

Answer: A.

If you keep recreating the same object and need only one, a singleton might be appropriate.

19.   How does the Singleton pattern relate to modular code design?

A. It's unrelated and cannot be used in modular code.

B. It can be used in combination with modules to provide a single instance of a resource module-wide.

C. It forces all modules to have their own singleton.

D. It breaks modular design.

Answer: B.

Singletons can be combined with modules to ensure a single instance per module or application.

20.　**Is the Singleton pattern considered a creational pattern?**

A. No, it is a behavioral pattern.

B. No, it is a structural pattern.

C. Yes, it is a creational pattern.

D. It's not a recognized pattern.

Answer: C.

The Singleton pattern is considered a creational pattern because it deals with object creation.

---

10 Coding Exercises with Full Solutions and Explanations

Exercise 1: Simple Singleton Getter

Task: Implement a singleton that returns an object with a random ID. Confirm that subsequent calls return the same object.

Solution:

```
var simpleSingleton = (function() {
    var instance;
    function createInstance() {
        return { id: Math.random() };
    }
    return {
        getInstance: function() {
            if (!instance) {
                instance = createInstance();
            }
            return instance;
        }
    };
})();


var s1 = simpleSingleton.getInstance();
var s2 = simpleSingleton.getInstance();
console.log(s1 === s2); // true
```

Explanation:

The closure stores a single instance. Once created, the same instance is returned.

Exercise 2: Logging Singleton

Task: Create a singleton logger that keeps an array of messages. Provide a log(message) method and a getLogs() method. Ensure all code gets the same instance.

Solution:

```
var logger = (function() {
    var instance;
    function createLogger() {
        var logs = [];
        return {
            log: function(msg) {
                logs.push(msg);
            },
            getLogs: function() {
                return logs.slice();
            }
        };
```

```javascript
        }
    return {
        getInstance: function() {
            if (!instance) {
                instance = createLogger();
            }
            return instance;
        }
    };
})();


var logger1 = logger.getInstance();
logger1.log("First log");
var logger2 = logger.getInstance();
logger2.log("Second log");
console.log(logger1.getLogs()); // ["First
log", "Second log"]
```

Explanation:
Both logger1 and logger2 point to the same instance,
sharing state.

Exercise 3: ES6 Class Singleton

Task: Create an ES6 class `Config` that only allows one instance. Add `get(key)` and `set(key, value)` methods. Demonstrate that multiple new `Config()` calls return the same instance.

Solution:

```
class Config {
    constructor() {
        if (Config.instance) {
            return Config.instance;
        }
        this.settings = {};
        Config.instance = this;
    }


    set(key, value) {
        this.settings[key] = value;
    }
```

```
    get(key) {
        return this.settings[key];
    }
}
```

```
const conf1 = new Config();
conf1.set("mode", "production");
```

```
const conf2 = new Config();
console.log(conf2.get("mode")); // "production"
console.log(conf1 === conf2); // true
```

Explanation:

`Config.instance` ensures `conf1` and `conf2` point to the same object.

Exercise 4: Database Connection Singleton

Task: Simulate a database connection as a singleton. The `connect()` method returns the same connection object every time, storing a `connectedAt` timestamp.

Solution:

```
var dbSingleton = (function() {
    var connection;


    function connect() {
        return {
            connectedAt: new Date()
        };
    }


    return {
        getConnection: function() {
            if (!connection) {
                connection = connect();
            }
            return connection;
        }
    };
})();
```

```
var dbc1 = dbSingleton.getConnection();
var dbc2 = dbSingleton.getConnection();
console.log(dbc1 === dbc2); // true
```

Explanation:

The connection variable is private. Once set, it stays the same.

Exercise 5: Cache Singleton

Task: Implement a cache singleton with set(key, value) and get(key). Show that retrieving the cache from different parts of the code returns the same data.
Solution:

```
var cacheSingleton = (function() {
    var cacheData = {};


    return {
        set: function(key, value) {
            cacheData[key] = value;
        },
```

```
        get: function(key) {
            return cacheData[key];
        }
    };
})();
```

```
cacheSingleton.set("token", "abc123");
console.log(cacheSingleton.get("token")); //
"abc123"
```

Explanation:

The module returns a single object. You can't create another instance of cacheSingleton.

Exercise 6: Singleton with Initialization Flag

Task: Create a singleton that has an init() method that sets a certain property. Subsequent calls to init() should not overwrite if already initialized.

Solution:

```
var initSingleton = (function() {
    var instance;
    function createInstance() {
        return { initialized: false, value:
null };
    }


    return {
        getInstance: function() {
            if (!instance) instance =
createInstance();
            return instance;
        },
        init: function(val) {
            var inst = this.getInstance();
            if (!inst.initialized) {
                inst.initialized = true;
                inst.value = val;
            }
        }
    };
})();
```

```
initSingleton.init("Start");
console.log(initSingleton.getInstance().value);
// "Start"
initSingleton.init("Another");
console.log(initSingleton.getInstance().value);
// still "Start"
```

Explanation:

We control initialization logic in the singleton to prevent multiple re-initializations.

Exercise 7: Singleton Counter

Task: Create a singleton counter with `increment()`, `decrement()`, and `getCount()` methods.
Solution:

```
var counterSingleton = (function() {
    var instance;
    function createCounter() {
        var count = 0;
```

```javascript
        return {
            increment: function() { count++; },
            decrement: function() { count--; },
            getCount: function() { return
count; }
        };
    }
    return {
        getInstance: function() {
            if (!instance) instance =
createCounter();
            return instance;
        }
    };
})();


var c1 = counterSingleton.getInstance();
c1.increment();
c1.increment();


var c2 = counterSingleton.getInstance();
c2.decrement();
```

```
console.log(c1.getCount()); // 1 (same
instance)
```

Explanation:

c1 and c2 share the same internal counter state.

Exercise 8: Singleton with Configuration Loading

Task: Create a singleton that "loads" some configuration from a mock object only once.

Solution:

```
var configLoaderSingleton = (function() {
    var instance;
    function loadConfig() {
        return { apiKey: "XYZ", env: "dev" };
    }
    return {
        getConfig: function() {
            if (!instance) {
                instance = loadConfig();
```

```
        }
        return instance;
    }
};
})();
```

```
console.log(configLoaderSingleton.getConfig());
// {apiKey: "XYZ", env: "dev"}
```

Explanation:
The config is loaded only once, subsequent calls return the cached config object.

Exercise 9: Singleton for Localization

Task: Create a singleton that stores a language setting. Add methods setLanguage(lang) and getLanguage().
Solution:

```
var localizationSingleton = (function() {
    var language = "en";
```

```
        return {
            setLanguage: function(lang) {
                language = lang;
            },
            getLanguage: function() {
                return language;
            }
        };
    })();


console.log(localizationSingleton.getLanguage()
); // "en"
localizationSingleton.setLanguage("fr");
console.log(localizationSingleton.getLanguage()
); // "fr"
```

Explanation:

Since we never return a constructor, this is just a single object. It's effectively a singleton.

Exercise 10: Singleton with Reset Method

Task: Create a singleton that maintains a `sessionID`. Provide `getSession()` to retrieve it, and `resetSession()` to create a new session.

Solution:

```
var sessionSingleton = (function() {
    var sessionID;
    function createSession() {
        return "session-" + Math.random();
    }
    return {
        getSession: function() {
            if (!sessionID) {
                sessionID = createSession();
            }
            return sessionID;
        },
        resetSession: function() {
            sessionID = createSession();
        }
    };
})();
```

```
console.log(sessionSingleton.getSession()); //
e.g. "session-0.12345"
sessionSingleton.resetSession();
console.log(sessionSingleton.getSession()); //
new session ID
```

Explanation:

We maintain a private `sessionID`. `resetSession()` creates a new unique session ID, but still through the singleton interface.

Conclusion

The Singleton pattern in JavaScript provides a way to ensure only one instance of a particular object exists. This can simplify state management and resource handling. However, it should be used judiciously since it can lead to global state management challenges and complicate testing.

By understanding how to implement singletons—whether with IIFEs, closures, or ES6 classes—you can apply this pattern where appropriate, such as for configuration management, logging utilities, or database connections. The code examples, questions, and exercises above will help you deepen your understanding and mastery of the Singleton pattern in JavaScript.

Introduction to the Observer Pattern

What is the Observer Pattern?

The Observer pattern is a software design pattern in which an object, known as the **subject** (or "observable"), maintains a list of its dependents, called **observers**, and notifies them automatically of any state changes, usually by calling one of their methods. In other words, it's a mechanism that allows different parts of a program to subscribe to certain events (or changes) and react when those events are triggered.

In JavaScript, the Observer pattern is commonly implemented using **event listeners and event emitters**. The subject (often called an **emitter**) can emit events. Observers (often called **listeners**) register callback functions that run when an event is emitted.

Why Use the Observer Pattern?

1.   **Loose Coupling**: Observers do not need to know details about the subject, and the subject does not need to know details about the observers. They just need to agree on the event names and data formats.

2.   **Extensibility**: It's easy to add or remove observers at runtime without modifying the subject.

3.   **Separation of Concerns**: Logic related to responding to events is encapsulated in observers. The subject focuses only on emitting events.

Key Concepts

•   **Subject (Observable/Emitter)**: The entity that sends out notifications (events).

•   **Observer (Listener/Subscriber)**: The entity that receives notifications and responds accordingly.

•   **Event**: A named signal that something has happened. Observers can subscribe to certain events.

Basic Implementation in JavaScript

JavaScript doesn't have a built-in Observer pattern class (until you consider libraries or APIs like EventTarget in the DOM), but it can be implemented using simple patterns:

- **DOM Events**: The browser DOM already implements an observer pattern with `addEventListener` and `removeEventListener`.
- **Custom Event Emitters**: Node.js includes a built-in `EventEmitter` class. For browsers, you can roll your own or use something like `EventTarget`.

Code Examples

Example 1: Simple Custom Event Emitter

```javascript
function EventEmitter() {
    this.events = {};
}



EventEmitter.prototype.on = function(eventName,
listener) {
    if (!this.events[eventName]) {
        this.events[eventName] = [];
    }
    this.events[eventName].push(listener);
```

```
};


EventEmitter.prototype.emit =
function(eventName, ...args) {
    if (this.events[eventName]) {
        this.events[eventName].forEach(listener
=> listener(...args));
    }
};


EventEmitter.prototype.off =
function(eventName, listener) {
    if (this.events[eventName]) {
        this.events[eventName] =
this.events[eventName].filter(fn => fn !==
listener);
    }
};


// Usage:
```

```
const emitter = new EventEmitter();
function greet(name) {
    console.log("Hello, " + name);
}
emitter.on("greet", greet);
emitter.emit("greet", "Alice"); // Hello, Alice
emitter.off("greet", greet);
emitter.emit("greet", "Bob"); // No output
```

Explanation:

- on(eventName, listener): Subscribes a listener to an event.
- emit(eventName, ...args): Notifies all listeners of an event.
- off(eventName, listener): Removes a specific listener.

Example 2: Using DOM Events as Observer Pattern

```
<button id="myButton">Click Me</button>
<script>
    const btn =
document.getElementById('myButton');
```

```
function handleClick() {
    console.log("Button was clicked!");
}
btn.addEventListener("click", handleClick);



// Later, you can remove the listener if
needed:
    // btn.removeEventListener("click",
handleClick);
</script>
```

Explanation:

addEventListener attaches a listener to an event (like "click") on a DOM element. When the event occurs, the listener is invoked. This is a direct application of the Observer pattern.

Example 3: Node.js EventEmitter

Node.js provides a built-in events module with EventEmitter.

```
const EventEmitter = require('events');
const myEmitter = new EventEmitter();


myEmitter.on('data', (info) => {
  console.log('Data event received:', info);
});


myEmitter.emit('data', { value: 42 });
// Output: Data event received: { value: 42 }
```

Explanation:

EventEmitter from Node.js is a classic observer pattern
implementation: you register callbacks with .on(), and trigger
events with .emit().

Example 4: Multiple Observers and Multiple Events

```
const emitter = new EventEmitter();


function firstListener() {
```

```
        console.log("First listener triggered.");
}
function secondListener() {
        console.log("Second listener triggered.");
}


emitter.on("update", firstListener);
emitter.on("update", secondListener);


emitter.emit("update");
// Output:
// First listener triggered.
// Second listener triggered.
```

Explanation:

You can have multiple observers for the same event. All will be notified when update is emitted.

Example 5: Once Listener

Some event systems allow a listener to be executed only once:

```javascript
EventEmitter.prototype.once =
function(eventName, listener) {
    const wrapper = (...args) => {
        listener(...args);
        this.off(eventName, wrapper);
    };
    this.on(eventName, wrapper);
};


// Usage:
const emitterOnce = new EventEmitter();
emitterOnce.once("ping", () =>
console.log("Ping received once!"));
emitterOnce.emit("ping"); // Ping received
once!
emitterOnce.emit("ping"); // No output
```

Multiple Choice Questions

1.   **What does the Observer Pattern achieve?**

A. Ensures only one instance of a class.

B. Allows an object to notify other objects of changes.

C. Provides a blueprint for creating objects.

D. None of the above.

Answer: B.

The Observer Pattern involves a subject notifying observers about changes.

2.   **In JavaScript, what commonly represents the "Subject" in the Observer Pattern?**

A. Math object

B. Event emitter

C. Array literal

D. JSON parser

Answer: B.

An event emitter (or similar construct) acts as the subject.

3.   **DOM event listeners follow which pattern?**

A. Singleton Pattern

B. Factory Pattern

C. Observer Pattern

D. Strategy Pattern

Answer: C.

83

`addEventListener` and `removeEventListener` implement the Observer Pattern.

4.   Which method adds a listener to an event in a custom emitter implementation?

A. `.push()`

B. `.listen()`

C. `.on()`

D. `.trigger()`

Answer: C.

Commonly, `.on()` is used to add a listener.

5.   Which method is typically used to trigger event notifications in an event emitter?

A. `.emit()`

B. `.dispatch()`

C. `.raise()`

D. `.notify()`

Answer: A.

`.emit()` is commonly used to fire events.

6.   Which built-in Node.js class implements the Observer Pattern?

A. `EventEmitter`

B. `Buffer`

C. `Path`

D. `Fs`

Answer: A.

EventEmitter is the Node.js implementation of the pattern.

7. **Why is the Observer Pattern useful?**

A. It tightly couples components.

B. It lets objects communicate without having to explicitly call each other's methods.

C. It forces synchronous code execution.

D. It is only used in front-end frameworks.

Answer: B.

Observer reduces coupling and lets observers react to events indirectly.

8. **If you no longer want a particular function to respond to an event, what should you do?**

A. Call `.off(eventName, listener)` or `.removeEventListener(eventName, listener)`.

B. Redefine the event emitter object.

C. Emit a "remove" event.

D. None of the above.

Answer: A.

Removing a listener requires an `.off()` or `.removeEventListener()` method.

9. **Which of these is NOT a key concept in the Observer Pattern?**

A. Subject (or Observable)

B. Observer (or Listener)

C. State Storage

D. Notification

Answer: C.

While a subject might have internal state, "state storage" is not a formal key concept. The pattern is about subjects and observers, and notifications.

10.   **What is a potential downside of using the Observer Pattern?**

A. It makes code completely unreadable.

B. If there are many events and observers, debugging can become more difficult.

C. It prevents all asynchronous code.

D. It never scales to large applications.

Answer: B.

Complex event systems can be harder to debug due to indirect notification flows.

11.   **In the DOM,**
`element.addEventListener('click', handler)` **is an example of:**

A. The element being an observer and handler being the subject.

B. The element being the subject and handler the observer.

C. Both element and handler are subjects.

D. Both are observers.

Answer: B.

The element (subject) notifies the handler (observer) on click events.

12. **How do you remove a listener in Node.js EventEmitter?**

A. `emitter.off(event, listener)` or `emitter.removeListener(event, listener)`

B. `emitter.kill(event)`

C. `emitter.stop(event, listener)`

D. `emitter.delete(event, listener)`

Answer: A.

`removeListener` or `off` can remove the listener in Node.js EventEmitter.

13. **Which pattern is essentially a publish/subscribe system at its core?**

A. Observer Pattern

B. Module Pattern

C. Singleton Pattern

D. Adapter Pattern

Answer: A.

The Observer Pattern is akin to publish/subscribe.

14. **Which method would you use in the EventEmitter class to trigger the event listeners?**

A. `.notify()`

B. `.emit()`

C. `.dispatchEvent()`

D. `.signal()`

Answer: B.

`.emit()` is the standard method to invoke registered listeners.

15.   **If no listeners are registered for an event and you call `.emit()` with that event name:**

A. It throws an error.

B. Nothing happens.

C. It logs a warning.

D. It automatically adds a default listener.

Answer: B.

Emitting an event with no listeners silently does nothing.

16.   **Which is a correct pattern to remove a DOM event listener?**

A. `element.removeEventListener('click', handler)`

B. `element.off('click', handler)`

C. `element.detachListener('click', handler)`

D. `element.stopListening('click', handler)`

Answer: A.

The standard DOM method is `removeEventListener`.

17.   **Can the Observer Pattern be used for asynchronous events?**

A. Yes, it is commonly used for asynchronous event handling in JavaScript.

B. No, it only works with synchronous calls.

C. Only in Node.js.

D. Only in the DOM.

Answer: A.

The Observer Pattern is frequently used in asynchronous event handling.

18.   If you want a handler to run only once for a certain event, you can:

A. Add it twice and remove one after it runs.

B. Use a `once` method if available, which removes the handler after the first invocation.

C. Call `.emitOnce()` instead of `.emit()`.

D. Use `.on()` but pass a special flag.

Answer: B.

`once` methods are common and remove the listener after it runs once.

19.   In a custom implementation of the Observer Pattern, what data structure often stores listeners?

A. Object or Map keyed by event names, with arrays of functions as values.

B. A global variable

C. A linked list of events

D. JSON file

Answer: A.

Typically, an object with keys as event names and arrays of callbacks as values.

20.   What is a major benefit of using events and observers in large applications?

A. It introduces strong coupling.

B. Components can react to events without hard-coded

89

dependencies, improving maintainability.

C. It ensures all code runs synchronously.

D. It forbids modularization.

Answer: B.

The pattern allows decoupled architecture, improving maintainability.

10 Coding Exercises with Full Solutions and Explanations

Exercise 1: Basic Event Emitter

Task: Implement a minimal EventEmitter class with on(event, fn) and emit(event, ...args) methods. Test it by registering a listener and emitting an event.

Solution:

```
class EventEmitter {
    constructor() {
        this.events = {};
    }
```

```
    on(event, fn) {
        if (!this.events[event])
this.events[event] = [];
        this.events[event].push(fn);
    }



    emit(event, ...args) {
        if (this.events[event]) {
            this.events[event].forEach(fn =>
fn(...args));
        }
    }
}



// Test
const emitter = new EventEmitter();
emitter.on("test", (msg) =>
console.log("Received:", msg));
emitter.emit("test", "Hello"); // Output:
"Received: Hello"
```

Explanation:

We store callbacks in `this.events`. Calling `emit` invokes all stored callbacks.

Exercise 2: Removing Listeners

Task: Extend the above EventEmitter with an `off(event, fn)` method to remove a specific listener.

Solution:

```
class EventEmitter {
    constructor() {
        this.events = {};
    }


    on(event, fn) {
        if (!this.events[event])
this.events[event] = [];
        this.events[event].push(fn);
    }
```

```javascript
  off(event, fn) {
    if (this.events[event]) {
      this.events[event] =
this.events[event].filter(listener => listener
!== fn);
    }
  }


  emit(event, ...args) {
    if (this.events[event]) {
      this.events[event].forEach(fn =>
fn(...args));
    }
  }
}


// Test
const emitter = new EventEmitter();
function greet(name) { console.log("Hello, " +
name); }
emitter.on("greet", greet);
```

```
emitter.emit("greet", "Alice"); // Hello, Alice
emitter.off("greet", greet);
emitter.emit("greet", "Bob"); // No output
```

Explanation:

off filters out the listener, stopping it from triggering.

Exercise 3: Once Method

Task: Add a once(event, fn) method that registers a
listener that removes itself after the first invocation.
Solution:

```
class EventEmitter {
    constructor() {
        this.events = {};
    }



    on(event, fn) {
        if (!this.events[event])
this.events[event] = [];
        this.events[event].push(fn);
```

```
}


off(event, fn) {
    if (this.events[event]) {
        this.events[event] =
this.events[event].filter(listener => listener
!== fn);
    }
}


once(event, fn) {
    const wrapper = (...args) => {
        fn(...args);
        this.off(event, wrapper);
    };
    this.on(event, wrapper);
}


emit(event, ...args) {
    if (this.events[event]) {
```

```
            this.events[event].forEach(fn =>
fn(...args));
        }
    }
}


// Test
const emitter = new EventEmitter();
emitter.once("ping", () => console.log("Ping
received once"));
emitter.emit("ping"); // "Ping received once"
emitter.emit("ping"); // No output
```

Explanation:

once uses a wrapper function that calls the original callback and then removes itself.

Exercise 4: Multiple Events Handling

Task: Create an emitter, register two different events ("start" and "end"), and verify that emitting one event does not trigger the other's listeners.

Solution:

```
const emitter = new EventEmitter();
emitter.on("start", () => console.log("Start
event"));
emitter.on("end", () => console.log("End
event"));


emitter.emit("start"); // Start event
emitter.emit("end");   // End event
```

Explanation:

Separate events have separate listener arrays.

Exercise 5: DOM Event as Observer Pattern

Task: Add a click listener to a button and log a message.
Remove the listener and test clicking again.

HTML:

```
<button id="btn">Click me</button>
<script>
    const btn = document.getElementById("btn");
    function handleClick() {
```

```
        console.log("Button clicked!");
    }
    btn.addEventListener("click", handleClick);
    // To remove:
    // btn.removeEventListener("click",
handleClick);
</script>
```

Explanation:
Standard DOM event handling demonstrates the Observer pattern.

Exercise 6: Event Emitter with Data

Task: Create an emitter, register a listener for "data" events, and emit a data object. The listener should log the received data.
Solution:

```
const dataEmitter = new EventEmitter();
dataEmitter.on("data", (payload) => {
    console.log("Data received:", payload);
});
dataEmitter.emit("data", { id: 1, value: 42 });
```

Explanation:

Observers can receive and process arbitrary data passed through emit.

Exercise 7: Chaining on/emit Methods

Task: Modify the EventEmitter's on() and emit() to return this so you can chain calls.

Solution:

```
class EventEmitter {
    constructor() {
        this.events = {};
    }



    on(event, fn) {
        if (!this.events[event])
this.events[event] = [];
        this.events[event].push(fn);
        return this; // enable chaining
    }
```

```
    off(event, fn) {
        if (this.events[event]) {
            this.events[event] =
this.events[event].filter(listener => listener
!== fn);
        }
        return this;
    }


    emit(event, ...args) {
        if (this.events[event]) {
            this.events[event].forEach(fn =>
fn(...args));
        }
        return this;
    }
}


// Test chaining:
const chainEmitter = new EventEmitter();
chainEmitter
```

```
.on("chain", (msg) => console.log(msg))
.emit("chain", "Chaining works!")
.emit("chain", "Hello again!");
```

Explanation:

By returning this, we can do

`emitter.on(...).emit(...).emit(...)`.

Exercise 8: Counting Listeners

Task: Add a `listenerCount(event)` method to return how many listeners are registered for a given event.
Solution:

```
class EventEmitter {
    constructor() {
        this.events = {};
    }


    on(event, fn) {
```

```
        if (!this.events[event])
this.events[event] = [];
        this.events[event].push(fn);
    }



    listenerCount(event) {
        return this.events[event] ?
this.events[event].length : 0;
    }



    emit(event, ...args) {
        if (this.events[event]) {
            this.events[event].forEach(fn =>
fn(...args));
        }
    }
}


// Test
const countEmitter = new EventEmitter();
countEmitter.on("hello", () => {});
```

```
countEmitter.on("hello", () => {});
console.log(countEmitter.listenerCount("hello")
); // 2
```

Explanation:

`listenerCount` helps monitor how many observers are attached.

Exercise 9: Namespaced Events

Task: Create a system where events can have namespaces, like "user:login". The `emit` should match full event names exactly.
Solution:

```
class EventEmitter {
    constructor() {
        this.events = {};
    }



    on(event, fn) {
```

```
        if (!this.events[event])
this.events[event] = [];
        this.events[event].push(fn);
    }



    emit(event, ...args) {
        if (this.events[event]) {
            this.events[event].forEach(fn =>
fn(...args));
        }
    }
}


// Test
const nsEmitter = new EventEmitter();
nsEmitter.on("user:login", user =>
console.log("User logged in:", user));
nsEmitter.emit("user:login", { name: "Alice"
}); // User logged in: { name: "Alice" }
```

Explanation:

The pattern remains the same; event names can include namespaces as strings.

Exercise 10: Logging All Emitted Events

Task: Modify the EventEmitter to have a `logAllEvents()` method that logs every event emitted. You can override `emit` to log the event name before notifying listeners.

Solution:

```
class EventEmitter {
    constructor() {
        this.events = {};
        this.logAll = false;
    }



    on(event, fn) {
        if (!this.events[event])
this.events[event] = [];
        this.events[event].push(fn);
    }
```

```
    logAllEvents(enable = true) {
        this.logAll = enable;
    }


    emit(event, ...args) {
        if (this.logAll) {
            console.log("Emitting event:",
event, "with args:", args);
        }
        if (this.events[event]) {
            this.events[event].forEach(fn =>
fn(...args));
        }
    }
}


// Test
const logEmitter = new EventEmitter();
logEmitter.logAllEvents(true);
logEmitter.on("debug", msg =>
console.log("Debug:", msg));
```

```
logEmitter.emit("debug", "Test message");
// Output:
// Emitting event: debug with args: [ 'Test
message' ]
// Debug: Test message
```

Explanation:

We track a boolean `logAll` to decide if we log each emitted event.

Conclusion

The Observer Pattern is a fundamental pattern for decoupled communication among different parts of a program. JavaScript provides multiple ways to implement it, from the native DOM event system to Node.js's `EventEmitter`, or custom implementations. Understanding how to implement, add, remove, and emit events gives you powerful tools to build responsive and modular applications. The above questions, examples, and exercises should help deepen your understanding and proficiency with the Observer Pattern in JavaScript.

Introduction to the Factory Pattern

What is the Factory Pattern?

The **Factory Pattern** is a creational design pattern that defines an interface or function for creating objects without specifying their exact classes. Instead of using a direct constructor call (e.g., new `ClassName()`), you use a special "factory" function or object that decides which specific instance of a class (or which object type) to create, often based on provided parameters or configuration.

This pattern decouples the object creation process from the code that uses the object, improving flexibility and maintainability. It's especially useful when you need to handle complex object creation logic, create different types of objects based on conditions, or hide the specifics of object construction from the rest of your code.

Why Use the Factory Pattern?

1.   **Encapsulation of Object Creation**: The factory method handles the creation logic in one place.

2.   **Abstraction**: Callers do not need to know the details of how objects are created or their classes.

3.   **Flexibility**: Easily switch out different object types without changing the calling code.

4.   **Maintainability**: Changes to object creation code are centralized, making your codebase easier to maintain.

Key Concepts

•   **Factory Function**: A function that returns new objects. It abstracts the new keyword and class details from the caller.

•   **Interface Decoupling**: The caller requests an object via the factory, and the factory decides which specific subtype to return.

When to Use?

•   When you have object creation code scattered throughout your codebase.

•   When you anticipate that the object you need might vary depending on some conditions.

•   When you want to avoid directly instantiating classes and prefer a more configurable approach.

Detailed Code Examples

Example 1: Simple Factory Function

```
function createPerson(name, age) {
    return {
        name,
        age,
        greet() {
            console.log(`Hello, my name is
${this.name}.`);
        }
    };
}


// Usage
const alice = createPerson("Alice", 30);
alice.greet(); // "Hello, my name is Alice."
```

Explanation:

Here, createPerson is a factory function that creates and

returns an object. The caller does not deal with new or a specific class; it just uses the factory.

Example 2: Factory Deciding Object Type

```
function carFactory(type) {
    if (type === "electric") {
        return { brand: "Tesla", fuel:
"electric" };
    } else if (type === "gas") {
        return { brand: "Toyota", fuel:
"gasoline" };
    } else {
        return { brand: "Generic", fuel:
"unknown" };
    }
}



// Usage
const eCar = carFactory("electric");
const gCar = carFactory("gas");
```

```
console.log(eCar); // {brand: "Tesla", fuel:
"electric"}
console.log(gCar); // {brand: "Toyota", fuel:
"gasoline"}
```

Explanation:

The carFactory decides what object to return based on the
type parameter.

Example 3: Factory with Constructor Functions

```
function Dog(name) {
    this.name = name;
    this.speak = function() {
console.log("Woof!"); };
}
```

```
function Cat(name) {
    this.name = name;
    this.speak = function() {
console.log("Meow!"); };
```

```
}


function animalFactory(type, name) {
    if (type === "dog") return new Dog(name);
    if (type === "cat") return new Cat(name);
    return null;
}


// Usage
const myDog = animalFactory("dog", "Rex");
const myCat = animalFactory("cat", "Whiskers");
myDog.speak(); // "Woof!"
myCat.speak(); // "Meow!"
```

Explanation:

The animalFactory chooses which constructor to use to create the object, abstracting this logic from the caller.

Example 4: ES6 Class-Based Factory

```
class Square {
    constructor(size) {
        this.size = size;
    }
    area() {
        return this.size * this.size;
    }
}


class Circle {
    constructor(radius) {
        this.radius = radius;
    }
    area() {
        return Math.PI * this.radius *
this.radius;
    }
}


function shapeFactory(shapeType, dimension) {
    if (shapeType === "square") return new
Square(dimension);
```

```
    if (shapeType === "circle") return new
Circle(dimension);
    return null;
}



// Usage
const mySquare = shapeFactory("square", 4);
console.log(mySquare.area()); // 16
const myCircle = shapeFactory("circle", 3);
console.log(myCircle.area()); // ~28.2743338823
```

Explanation:

The factory function chooses which class to instantiate based on shapeType.

Example 5: Configurable Factory

```
function userFactory(userData) {
    const baseUser = {
        name: userData.name,
        role: userData.role,
```

```javascript
        info() {
            console.log(`${this.name} is a
${this.role}`);
        }
    };


    if (userData.role === "admin") {
        baseUser.manageUsers = function() {
            console.log("Managing users...");
        };
    }


    return baseUser;
}


// Usage
const adminUser = userFactory({ name: "Alice",
role: "admin" });
const regularUser = userFactory({ name: "Bob",
role: "user" });
```

```
adminUser.info(); // Alice is a admin
adminUser.manageUsers(); // Managing users...
regularUser.info(); // Bob is a user
// regularUser.manageUsers(); // undefined
```

Explanation:
The factory logic modifies the returned object's capabilities based on input parameters.

Multiple Choice Questions

1   **The Factory Pattern is mainly used to:** A. Directly instantiate objects using new `ClassName()`. B. Encapsulate object creation logic and return different objects based on conditions.
C. Create global variables.
D. Replace all classes with functions.
Answer: B.
The Factory Pattern encapsulates object creation, often returning different objects depending on input.
2.   **In JavaScript, a factory is often implemented as:** A. A class with a static `create()` method.

117

B. A simple function that returns objects.

C. A global variable.

D. A DOM event handler.

Answer: B.

Commonly, factories are simple functions that return objects.

3.   **A key advantage of using the Factory Pattern is:** A. Tight coupling between creator and created objects.

B. Centralized object creation logic, improving maintainability.

C. Mandatory use of the new keyword.

D. Limiting code reuse.

Answer: B.

Factories centralize and manage object creation logic, making the code more maintainable.

4.   **Which scenario is a good fit for the Factory Pattern?**

A. You have only one simple object type that never changes.

B. You have multiple object types and want to choose one at runtime without changing the calling code.

C. You want to get rid of objects entirely.

D. You don't want to create any objects.

Answer: B.

Factories shine when multiple object types might be created dynamically based on conditions.

5.   **The Factory Pattern helps avoid:** A. Abstracting complexities.

B. Reusing code.

C. Hard-coded references to specific classes throughout the code.

D. Using conditional logic.

Answer: C.

Instead of scattering new calls, you have a single place that decides which class/object to create.

6.   **Which is NOT a characteristic of the Factory Pattern?**

A. It provides a single point of object creation.

B. It increases coupling between the creator and the client code.

C. It can hide the complexity of the object creation.

D. It can return different types of objects.

Answer: B.

The Factory Pattern typically reduces coupling, not increases it.

7.   **In ES6+, which approach can you use for a factory?**

A. An arrow function returning different class instances.

B. Only function declarations.

C. You must use the `class` keyword.

D. None of the above.

Answer: A.

Any function (including arrow functions) can be used as a factory function.

8.   **If you have a factory function that returns different objects based on input, the calling code:** A. Must know the exact class name.

B. Doesn't need to know how objects are created.

C. Must specify the constructor arguments exactly.

D. Will break if you add new object types.

Answer: B.

The calling code just requests an object; it doesn't need to know the details.

9. **Which pattern category does the Factory Pattern belong to?** A. Structural

B. Behavioral

C. Creational

D. Concurrency

Answer: C.

The Factory Pattern is a creational design pattern.

10. **Factories can help with:** A. Enforcing the use of a single object instance.

B. Differentiating objects at runtime without changing the code that uses them.

C. Removing the need for all classes.

D. Preventing object creation completely.

Answer: B.

Factories let you decide which object to create at runtime.

11. **In a factory function, what is a common approach to decide which object to create?** A. Using conditional statements (if/else or switch) based on input parameters.

B. Random number generation.

C. Only returning null.

D. Hard-coding a single object type.

Answer: A.

Factories often use conditionals to choose which object to return.

12. **The Factory Pattern can be combined with other patterns. For example:** A. Singleton + Factory to manage unique instances.

B. Adapter + Factory to convert interfaces during creation.

C. Abstract Factory pattern to create families of related objects.

D. All of the above.

Answer: D.

The Factory Pattern can be mixed with other patterns like Singleton, Adapter, and Abstract Factory.

13. **If a factory returns null, it typically means:** A. An unsupported type or condition was requested.

B. Everything is working perfectly.

C. The factory forgot to return something.

D. The factory is not needed.

Answer: A.

Returning null usually indicates an invalid input or unsupported request.

14. **One disadvantage of the Factory Pattern could be:** A. Centralized code can become a maintenance hotspot if not organized well.

B. It solves all architectural problems.

C. It reduces the number of classes needed.

D. It can't be tested.

Answer: A.

While centralizing creation is good, too much logic in one place can become cumbersome if not managed well.

15.   **Which of these is true about factory functions in JavaScript?** A. They must always use new.

B. They can return plain objects, no new required.

C. They must only return built-in objects.

D. They can't use conditionals.

Answer: B.

Factory functions often return plain objects created using object literals, without new.

16.   **A factory might be chosen over directly using constructors because:** A. It hides complex construction logic.

B. It forces the use of global variables.

C. It removes the need for parameters.

D. It breaks encapsulation.

Answer: A.

Factories can hide complexity and vary what gets created without exposing details.

17.   **When you want to easily add new product types to your code without changing the calling code, a factory:** A. Is less useful.

B. Can make it simpler by just adding a new condition in the factory.

C. Forces you to change all the client code.

D. Prevents any additions.

Answer: B.

Just update the factory function; the client code remains the same.

18. **In a factory pattern, the client code:** A. Knows exactly which subclass it gets.

B. Only knows it gets a valid object that meets certain criteria.

C. Must create the objects itself.

D. Must handle all initialization.

Answer: B.

The client trusts the factory to provide the right kind of object.

19. **Factories are especially useful in:** A. Large codebases where different object types might be introduced over time.

B. Very small scripts that never change.

C. Situations where no objects are ever created.

D. Scenarios with no variability in object creation.

Answer: A.

As code grows and evolves, factories are more beneficial.

20. **One reason to return objects from a factory rather than a class instance directly is:** A. You can't create class instances in JavaScript.

B. You can create objects with specific functionalities dynamically, no class needed.

C. It's illegal to use classes.

D. It prevents the use of prototypes.

Answer: B.

Factories offer flexibility to create objects in various ways without strictly using classes.

10 Coding Exercises with Full Solutions and Explanations

Exercise 1: Basic Object Factory

Task: Create a factory function `personFactory(name, age)` that returns a person object with those properties and a `greet()` method.

Solution:

```
function personFactory(name, age) {
    return {
        name,
        age,
        greet() {
            console.log(`Hi, I'm ${this.name}
and I'm ${this.age} years old.`);
        }
    };
}


// Test
```

```
const p = personFactory("Alice", 30);
p.greet(); // Hi, I'm Alice and I'm 30 years
old.
```

Explanation:
The factory returns a simple object with a greeting method. No classes needed.

Exercise 2: Conditional Object Creation

Task: Create a vehicleFactory(type) that returns an object {type} and a move() method that logs different messages depending on whether type is "car" or "boat".
Solution:

```
function vehicleFactory(type) {
    const vehicle = { type };
    if (type === "car") {
        vehicle.move = () => console.log("The
car drives on roads.");
    } else if (type === "boat") {
```

```
        vehicle.move = () => console.log("The
boat sails on water.");
    } else {
        vehicle.move = () =>
console.log("Unknown vehicle type.");
    }
    return vehicle;
}


// Test
const car = vehicleFactory("car");
car.move(); // The car drives on roads.
const boat = vehicleFactory("boat");
boat.move(); // The boat sails on water.
```

Explanation:

The factory assigns a move() method differently depending on type.

Exercise 3: Using Constructors in a Factory

Task: Define a Computer constructor and a Phone constructor. Then create a deviceFactory(type, brand) that returns a new `Computer(brand)` if type is "computer" and new `Phone(brand)` if type is "phone".

Solution:

```javascript
function Computer(brand) {
    this.brand = brand;
    this.describe = function() {
        console.log(`This is a ${this.brand} computer.`);
    };
}


function Phone(brand) {
    this.brand = brand;
    this.describe = function() {
        console.log(`This is a ${this.brand} phone.`);
    };
}
```

```
function deviceFactory(type, brand) {
    if (type === "computer") return new
Computer(brand);
    if (type === "phone") return new
Phone(brand);
    return null;
}



// Test
const myPC = deviceFactory("computer", "Dell");
myPC.describe(); // This is a Dell computer.
const myMobile = deviceFactory("phone",
"Apple");
myMobile.describe(); // This is a Apple phone.
```

Explanation:
We leverage constructors inside the factory.

Exercise 4: Flexible Factory with Defaults

Task: Create a shapeFactory(shape, dimension) that
returns a square with size = dimension if shape = "square",
and a circle with radius = dimension if shape = "circle". If

shape is not recognized, return a default object with a type =
"unknown" and a describe() method that logs "Unknown
shape."
Solution:

```
function shapeFactory(shape, dimension) {
    if (shape === "square") {
        return {
            type: "square",
            size: dimension,
            describe() { console.log(`A square
with size ${this.size}`); }
        };
    } else if (shape === "circle") {
        return {
            type: "circle",
            radius: dimension,
            describe() { console.log(`A circle
with radius ${this.radius}`); }
        };
    }
    return {
```

```
        type: "unknown",
        describe() { console.log("Unknown
shape"); }
    };
}
```

```
// Test
const s = shapeFactory("square", 4);
s.describe(); // A square with size 4
const c = shapeFactory("circle", 3);
c.describe(); // A circle with radius 3
const u = shapeFactory("triangle", 5);
u.describe(); // Unknown shape
```

Explanation:
The factory provides a safe fallback for unknown input.

Exercise 5: Adding Methods Conditionally

Task: Create userFactory(role) that returns an object with role. If role is "admin", add a method deleteUser() that logs "User deleted". If role is "guest", add a method requestAccess() that logs "Access requested".

Solution:

```javascript
function userFactory(role) {
    const user = { role };
    if (role === "admin") {
        user.deleteUser = () =>
console.log("User deleted");
    } else if (role === "guest") {
        user.requestAccess = () =>
console.log("Access requested");
    }
    return user;
}


// Test
const admin = userFactory("admin");
admin.deleteUser(); // User deleted
const guest = userFactory("guest");
guest.requestAccess(); // Access requested
```

Explanation:

The returned object's methods depend on the provided role.

Exercise 6: Complex Object Creation from Config

Task: Create a widgetFactory(config) that takes a config object with properties type and color. If type is "button", return an object with type, color, and click() method. If type is "text", return an object with type, color, and render() method that logs "Rendering text in {color} color".
Solution:

```
function widgetFactory(config) {
    if (config.type === "button") {
        return {
            type: "button",
            color: config.color,
            click() { console.log(`Button
clicked. Color: ${this.color}`); }
        };
    } else if (config.type === "text") {
        return {
            type: "text",
            color: config.color,
```

```javascript
      render() { console.log(`Rendering
text in ${this.color} color`); }
      };
   }
   return { type: "unknown" };
}


// Test
const btn = widgetFactory({ type: "button",
color: "blue" });
btn.click(); // Button clicked. Color: blue


const txt = widgetFactory({ type: "text",
color: "red" });
txt.render(); // Rendering text in red color
```

Explanation:
The factory uses a config object to decide what to create.

Exercise 7: Factory Returning Promises

Task: Create a dataFactory(source) that if source =
"remote", returns an object with a fetchData() method that
returns a Promise resolved with "Remote data". If source =
"local", return an object with a fetchData() method that
returns a Promise resolved with "Local data".
Solution:

```
function dataFactory(source) {
    if (source === "remote") {
        return {
            fetchData() {
                return Promise.resolve("Remote
data");
            }
        };
    } else if (source === "local") {
        return {
            fetchData() {
                return Promise.resolve("Local
data");
            }
        };
```

```
        }
    return {
        fetchData() {
            return Promise.reject("Unknown
source");
        }
    };
}


// Test
const remoteData = dataFactory("remote");
remoteData.fetchData().then(console.log); //
"Remote data"


const localData = dataFactory("local");
localData.fetchData().then(console.log); //
"Local data"
```

Explanation:

The factory can return objects that handle asynchronous operations differently.

Exercise 8: Abstracting Class Names

Task: Suppose you have two classes `MySQLConnection` and `PostgresConnection`. Create a `dbFactory(type)` that returns a new instance of the appropriate class based on `type = "mysql"` or `type = "postgres"`.

Solution:

```
class MySQLConnection {
    connect() { console.log("Connected to
MySQL"); }
}
```

```
class PostgresConnection {
    connect() { console.log("Connected to
PostgreSQL"); }
}
```

```
function dbFactory(type) {
```

```
    if (type === "mysql") return new
MySQLConnection();
    if (type === "postgres") return new
PostgresConnection();
    return null;
}



// Test
const mysql = dbFactory("mysql");
mysql.connect(); // Connected to MySQL


const pg = dbFactory("postgres");
pg.connect(); // Connected to PostgreSQL
```

Explanation:

The factory hides which class is instantiated.

Exercise 9: Extensible Factory

Task: Implement a animalFactory(type) that, by default, supports "dog" and "cat". If the given type isn't supported,

137

return a default animal that just logs "Unknown animal". Ensure it's easy to add new animals by changing only the factory.

Solution:

```
function animalFactory(type) {
    const animals = {
        dog: { type: "dog", sound() {
console.log("Woof"); } },
        cat: { type: "cat", sound() {
console.log("Meow"); } }
    };
    return animals[type] || { type: "unknown",
sound() { console.log("Unknown animal"); } };
}


// Test
const aDog = animalFactory("dog");
aDog.sound(); // Woof
const aCat = animalFactory("cat");
aCat.sound(); // Meow
const aFox = animalFactory("fox");
aFox.sound(); // Unknown animal
```

Explanation:

We used a lookup object to easily add new animals without changing calling code.

Exercise 10: Factory with Logging

Task: Create a `loggerFactory(level)` that returns an object with a `log(msg)` method. If `level = "info"`, prepend "[INFO]" to msg. If `level = "warn"`, prepend "[WARN]". If `level` is unknown, prepend "[LOG]".

Solution:

```
function loggerFactory(level) {
    return {
        log(msg) {
            if (level === "info") {
                console.log(`[INFO] ${msg}`);
            } else if (level === "warn") {
                console.warn(`[WARN] ${msg}`);
            } else {
                console.log(`[LOG] ${msg}`);
            }
```

```
      }
   };
}
```

```
// Test
const infoLogger = loggerFactory("info");
infoLogger.log("This is an info message."); //
[INFO] This is an info message.
```

```
const warnLogger = loggerFactory("warn");
warnLogger.log("This is a warning."); // [WARN]
This is a warning.
```

```
const defaultLogger = loggerFactory("debug");
defaultLogger.log("This is a default log."); //
[LOG] This is a default log.
```

Explanation:

We adapted the returned object's behavior based on the level parameter.

Conclusion

The Factory Pattern in JavaScript provides a systematic way to create objects, abstracting and centralizing the object creation process. By decoupling the client code from the specifics of the objects they need, factories make the system more flexible, maintainable, and easier to scale. The code examples, multiple-choice questions, and exercises above offer a solid understanding and practical experience with the Factory Pattern.

JavaScript: Prototype Pattern (Object-Based Inheritance)

The **Prototype Pattern** is a key concept in JavaScript, allowing objects to share properties and methods through a shared prototype. This is a fundamental principle in JavaScript's inheritance model and forms the backbone of how objects inherit from one another.

Introduction to the Prototype Pattern

The **Prototype Pattern** allows you to create new objects that inherit properties and methods from a prototype object. It enables reuse of existing objects as templates for new objects. This approach reduces memory usage and makes inheritance more efficient.

How Prototypes Work in JavaScript

Every JavaScript object has an internal property called `[[Prototype]]`, which can be accessed using `Object.getPrototypeOf(obj)` or `obj.__proto__`. When you access a property or method on an object, JavaScript will search the object itself. If it doesn't find it, it looks up the prototype chain.

Creating Prototypes

There are several ways to create prototypes in JavaScript:

Using `Object.create()`

```
const animal = {
  type: 'mammal',
  sound() {
    console.log('Generic animal sound');
  }
};
```

```
const dog = Object.create(animal);
dog.bark = function() {
  console.log('Woof!');
};
```

```
dog.sound(); // Output: Generic animal sound
(inherited from animal)
dog.bark();  // Output: Woof! (defined on dog)
```

Using Constructor Functions

```
function Animal(type) {
  this.type = type;
}
```

```
Animal.prototype.sound = function() {
  console.log('Generic animal sound');
};
```

```
const dog = new Animal('mammal');
dog.sound(); // Output: Generic animal sound
```

Using ES6 Classes

```
class Animal {
  constructor(type) {
    this.type = type;
  }
```

```
  sound() {
    console.log('Generic animal sound');
  }
}


class Dog extends Animal {
  bark() {
    console.log('Woof!');
  }
}


const dog = new Dog('mammal');
dog.sound(); // Output: Generic animal sound
dog.bark();  // Output: Woof!
```

Prototype Chain

The prototype chain is a series of links between objects. When you try to access a property on an object, JavaScript follows this chain to look for the property.

Example:

```
const grandparent = { a: 1 };
const parent = Object.create(grandparent);
const child = Object.create(parent);


console.log(child.a); // Output: 1 (found in
grandparent)
```

Prototype Inheritance

Prototypes allow objects to inherit properties and methods from other objects.

Example:

```
function Person(name) {
  this.name = name;
}



Person.prototype.greet = function() {
  console.log(`Hello, my name is
${this.name}`);
};



const john = new Person('John');
john.greet(); // Output: Hello, my name is John
```

Advantages of the Prototype Pattern

• **Memory Efficient:** Methods are shared between instances, so memory usage is lower.
• **Dynamic Inheritance:** Properties and methods can be modified after object creation.

- **Chainable Inheritance:** Objects can inherit properties through multiple levels of prototypes.

Disadvantages of the Prototype Pattern

- **Hard to Debug:** Since properties are inherited, it's sometimes hard to know where a property is coming from.
- **Confusion with this:** The value of this can be confusing, especially with nested functions or event listeners.

Examples and Use Cases

- **Creating Multiple Instances**: Avoids duplicating methods for every instance.
- **Shared Functionality**: Shared methods are defined on prototypes, making code DRY.
- **Custom Inheritance Chains**: Custom objects can inherit from other objects.

Multiple Choice Questions with Answers

Question 1

Which method is used to create a new object with a specified prototype?

- A) `Object.create()`
- B) `Object.prototype()`
- C) `new Object()`
- D) `Object.assign()`

Answer: A) `Object.create()`

Explanation: `Object.create()` creates a new object with the specified prototype.

Question 2

What does `Object.getPrototypeOf(obj)` return?

- A) The parent object of `obj`
- B) The prototype of `obj`
- C) The constructor of `obj`
- D) None of the above

Answer: B) The prototype of `obj`

Explanation: `Object.getPrototypeOf(obj)` returns the internal `[[Prototype]]` of `obj`.

Question 3

Which of the following correctly sets up prototype inheritance?
- **A)** `const obj = Object.inherit(parentObj);`
- **B)** `const obj = new parentObj();`
- **C)** `const obj = Object.create(parentObj);`
- **D)** `const obj = Object.extends(parentObj);`

Answer: C) `const obj = Object.create(parentObj);`

Explanation: The correct method to set up prototype inheritance in JavaScript is `Object.create()`, which creates a new object with the prototype set to `parentObj`.

Question 4

What will the following code output?

```
function Dog(name) {
  this.name = name;
}
```

```
Dog.prototype.bark = function() {
  console.log('Woof!');
};


const dog1 = new Dog('Buddy');
dog1.bark();
```

- **A)** Error
- **B)** Woof!
- **C)** Buddy
- **D)** Undefined

Answer: B) Woof!

Explanation: The bark method is part of Dog.prototype, and dog1 inherits from this prototype. Hence, calling dog1.bark() will print Woof!.

Question 5

Which of the following will correctly check if `obj` has an own property name?

- **A)** `obj.name !== undefined`
- **B)** `'name' in obj`
- **C)** `obj.hasOwnProperty('name')`
- **D)** `Object.has(obj, 'name')`

Answer: C) `obj.hasOwnProperty('name')`

Explanation: `hasOwnProperty()` checks if the property is a direct (own) property of the object, not one inherited from its prototype.

Question 6

What is the prototype of a newly created array?

- **A)** `Object.prototype`
- **B)** `Array.prototype`
- **C)** `Function.prototype`
- **D)** `null`

Answer: B) `Array.prototype`

Explanation: Arrays in JavaScript inherit from `Array.prototype`, which itself inherits from `Object.prototype`.

Question 7

Which of the following best describes the prototype chain?

- **A)** A chain of functions
- **B)** A linked list of parent-child objects
- **C)** A list of static methods
- **D)** None of the above

Answer: B) A linked list of parent-child objects

Explanation: The prototype chain is a linked list of objects where each object inherits properties and methods from its parent (prototype) until `null` is reached.

Question 8

Which method returns the prototype of an object?

- **A)** `Object.getPrototypeOf(obj)`
- **B)** `obj.prototype`
- **C)** `obj.__proto__`
- **D)** Both A and C

Answer: D) Both A and C

Explanation: `Object.getPrototypeOf(obj)` and `obj.__proto__` both return the prototype of `obj`.

Question 9

What is the output of the following code?

```
function Animal() {}
Animal.prototype.legs = 4;


const cat = new Animal();
cat.legs = 3;


console.log(cat.legs);
```

- **A)** 3
- **B)** 4
- **C)** undefined
- **D)** Error

Answer: A) 3

Explanation: The property `legs` = 3 is an own property of `cat`, so it takes precedence over the property in `Animal.prototype`.

Question 10

Which of the following methods can be used to copy properties from one object to another?

- **A)** `Object.create()`
- **B)** `Object.assign()`
- **C)** `Object.clone()`
- **D)** None of the above

Answer: B) Object.assign()

Explanation: `Object.assign()` copies the properties of one or more source objects to a target object.

Coding Exercises with Full Solutions

Exercise 1: Object Inheritance

Create a prototype chain where `car` inherits from `vehicle`, and `electricCar` inherits from `car`.

Solution:

```
const vehicle = {
  start() {
    console.log('Vehicle starting...');
  }
};
```

```
const car = Object.create(vehicle);
car.drive = function() {
  console.log('Car is driving...');
};
```

```
const electricCar = Object.create(car);
electricCar.charge = function() {
  console.log('Electric car charging...');
```

```
};
```

```
electricCar.start();   // Output: Vehicle
starting...
electricCar.drive();   // Output: Car is
driving...
electricCar.charge(); // Output: Electric car
charging...
```

Exercise 2: Using Constructor Functions

Create a constructor function Person that initializes name and age, and add a greet method to the prototype.

Solution:

```
function Person(name, age) {
  this.name = name;
  this.age = age;
}
```

```
Person.prototype.greet = function() {
  console.log(`Hello, my name is ${this.name}
and I am ${this.age} years old.`);
};
```

```
const john = new Person('John', 25);
john.greet(); // Output: Hello, my name is John
and I am 25 years old.
```

Exercise 3: Check Prototype Chain

Write a function to check if one object is a prototype of another.
Solution:

```
function isPrototypeOf(obj, prototype) {
  return prototype.isPrototypeOf(obj);
}
```

```
const animal = { type: 'mammal' };
const dog = Object.create(animal);


console.log(isPrototypeOf(dog, animal)); //
Output: true
```

Exercise 4: Use `Object.create()`

Create an object person with a prototype method speak.
Solution:

```
const person = {
  speak() {
    console.log('Hello, I can speak!');
  }
};


const student = Object.create(person);
```

```
student.speak(); // Output: Hello, I can speak!
```

Exercise 5: Method Overriding

Override a prototype method.
Solution:

```javascript
function Person(name) {
  this.name = name;
}


Person.prototype.greet = function() {
  console.log('Hello');
};


const student = new Person('John');


student.greet = function() {
  console.log('Hello, I am a student.');
```

```
};
```

```
student.greet(); // Output: Hello, I am a
student.
```

Exercise 6: Custom Prototypes

Create an object with a custom prototype and inherit from it.
Solution:

```
const animal = {
  species: 'mammal',
  makeSound() {
    console.log('Animal sound');
  }
};
```

```
const dog = Object.create(animal);
dog.bark = function() {
```

```
  console.log('Woof!');
};
```

```
dog.makeSound(); // Output: Animal sound
dog.bark();      // Output: Woof!
```

Exercise 7: Object Inheritance

Task: Create a Vehicle prototype with move and stop methods. Then create a Car object that inherits from Vehicle and has an additional method honk.

Solution:

```
const Vehicle = {
  move() {
    console.log('Vehicle is moving...');
  },
  stop() {
    console.log('Vehicle stopped.');
  }
```

```
};
```

```
const Car = Object.create(Vehicle);
Car.honk = function() {
  console.log('Beep Beep!');
};
```

```
Car.move(); // Output: Vehicle is moving...
Car.honk(); // Output: Beep Beep!
Car.stop(); // Output: Vehicle stopped.
```

Exercise 8: Constructor Function

Task: Create a Book constructor function that accepts a title
and author. Add a prototype method getDetails.
Solution:

```
function Book(title, author) {
```

```
  this.title = title;
  this.author = author;
}
```

```
Book.prototype.getDetails = function() {
  return `${this.title} by ${this.author}`;
};
```

```
const book1 = new Book('1984', 'George
Orwell');
console.log(book1.getDetails()); // Output:
1984 by George Orwell
```

Exercise 9: Override Prototype Methods

Task: Override the toString method for an object.
Solution:

```
const person = {
  name: 'John',
```

```
  age: 30,
  toString() {
    return `${this.name}, Age: ${this.age}`;
  }
};
```

```
console.log(person.toString()); // Output:
John, Age: 30
```

Exercise 10: Custom Inheritance

Task: Create a Student object that inherits from Person and adds a study method.
Solution:

```
function Person(name) {
  this.name = name;
}
```

```javascript
Person.prototype.greet = function() {
  console.log(`Hello, my name is
${this.name}`);
};


function Student(name, course) {
  Person.call(this, name);
  this.course = course;
}


Student.prototype =
Object.create(Person.prototype);
Student.prototype.constructor = Student;


Student.prototype.study = function() {
  console.log(`${this.name} is studying
${this.course}`);
};


const student1 = new Student('Alice', 'Math');
```

```
student1.greet();   // Output: Hello, my name is
Alice
student1.study();   // Output: Alice is studying
Math
```

Exercise 11: Prototype Chain

Task: Create a prototype chain with grandparent, parent, and child.
Solution:

```
const grandparent - { property1: 'A' };
const parent = Object.create(grandparent);
const child = Object.create(parent);


console.log(child.property1); // Output: A
```

Exercise 12: Shared Methods

Task: Share methods between all objects of a specific type using a prototype.

Solution:

```
function Animal(type) {
  this.type = type;
}


Animal.prototype.makeSound = function() {
  console.log(`${this.type} makes a sound.`);
};


const dog = new Animal('Dog');
const cat = new Animal('Cat');


dog.makeSound(); // Output: Dog makes a sound.
cat.makeSound(); // Output: Cat makes a sound.
```

JavaScript: Strategy Pattern (Changing Behavior of Objects at Runtime)

The **Strategy Pattern** is one of the most commonly used design patterns in JavaScript. It allows you to define a family of algorithms, encapsulate each one in a separate class or function, and make them interchangeable at runtime. This pattern is particularly useful when you want to change an object's behavior without modifying its structure.

Introduction to the Strategy Pattern

The **Strategy Pattern** defines a family of interchangeable algorithms, encapsulates each one, and makes them interchangeable at runtime. This pattern allows the behavior of an object to change dynamically, making it more flexible and easier to maintain.

How the Strategy Pattern Works

The pattern involves three main parts:

- **Context**: This is the main object whose behavior will be changed at runtime.
- **Strategy**: The different strategies (algorithms) that can be applied to the context.
- **Concrete Strategies**: The actual implementations of the strategies.

Simple Conceptual Example: Imagine a payment system where users can pay using a credit card, PayPal, or cryptocurrency. You can create a `PaymentContext` class that allows users to choose a payment strategy at runtime.

Implementing the Strategy Pattern

Example 1: Payment System

```
// Step 1: Create different strategy functions
const CreditCardPayment = {
  pay: function(amount) {
    console.log(`Paid $${amount} using Credit
Card.`);
```

```
  }
};


const PayPalPayment = {
  pay: function(amount) {
    console.log(`Paid $${amount} using
PayPal.`);
  }
};


const CryptoPayment = {
  pay: function(amount) {
    console.log(`Paid $${amount} using
Cryptocurrency.`);
  }
};


// Step 2: Create the Context that can switch
between strategies
function PaymentContext(paymentStrategy) {
```

```
  this.paymentStrategy = paymentStrategy;
}


PaymentContext.prototype.setStrategy =
function(paymentStrategy) {
  this.paymentStrategy = paymentStrategy;
};


PaymentContext.prototype.pay = function(amount)
{
  this.paymentStrategy.pay(amount);
};


// Step 3: Use the Context to dynamically
change behavior
const payment = new
PaymentContext(CreditCardPayment);
payment.pay(100); // Output: Paid $100 using
Credit Card.
```

```
payment.setStrategy(PayPalPayment);
payment.pay(200); // Output: Paid $200 using
PayPal.
```

```
payment.setStrategy(CryptoPayment);
payment.pay(300); // Output: Paid $300 using
Cryptocurrency.
```

When to Use the Strategy Pattern

- **When you have multiple variations of the same behavior** (like different payment methods).
- **When you want to avoid conditionals (like switch-case or if-else chains)**.
- **When you want to separate logic into smaller, more maintainable pieces**.

Advantages and Disadvantages

Advantages

- **Cleaner Code**: Reduces large switch statements or conditionals.
- **Encapsulation**: Different algorithms are encapsulated in separate functions/objects.
- **Easy to Extend**: New strategies can be added without modifying existing code.

Disadvantages

- **Complexity**: Too many strategy classes might make the code harder to read.
- **Overhead**: Context objects and multiple strategy classes may increase memory usage.

Examples and Use Cases

- **Payment Systems**: Different payment methods (Credit Card, PayPal, Cryptocurrency, etc.).
- **Data Compression**: Switching between different compression algorithms at runtime.

- **Sorting Algorithms**: Switching between QuickSort, MergeSort, or BubbleSort at runtime.

Multiple Choice Questions with Answers

Question 1

Which of the following best describes the Strategy Pattern?
- **A)** It allows for dynamic method dispatch at runtime.
- **B)** It defines a family of algorithms and makes them interchangeable at runtime.
- **C)** It enforces a single responsibility principle.
- **D)** It creates an abstract factory of methods.

Answer: B) It defines a family of algorithms and makes them interchangeable at runtime.

Question 2

Which of the following is NOT a component of the Strategy Pattern?
- **A)** Context

- **B)** Strategy
- **C)** Singleton
- **D)** Concrete Strategy

Answer: C) Singleton

Question 3

Which method allows you to change the strategy at runtime?

- **A)** Use `Object.assign()`
- **B)** Change the strategy in the context
- **C)** Use `this.bind()`
- **D)** Modify the prototype of the context

Answer: B) Change the strategy in the context

Question 4

Which of the following best represents the role of the **Context** in the Strategy Pattern?

- **A)** Provides an interface for creating objects.
- **B)** Provides a way to swap strategies at runtime.
- **C)** Encapsulates multiple algorithms.
- **D)** Ensures objects are created with default properties.

Answer: B) Provides a way to swap strategies at runtime.

Question 5

What is the purpose of the **Strategy** in the Strategy Pattern?

- **A)** It represents the concrete implementation.
- **B)** It defines the interface for a family of interchangeable algorithms.
- **C)** It is a static method of a class.
- **D)** It allows the use of inheritance instead of composition.

Answer: B) It defines the interface for a family of interchangeable algorithms.

Question 6

How do you create a new strategy for a context?

- **A)** Modify the constructor.
- **B)** Create a new strategy function and attach it to the context.
- **C)** Add a method to the prototype of the context.
- **D)** Use `Object.setPrototypeOf()`.

Answer: B) Create a new strategy function and attach it to the context.

Question 7

What is the main benefit of the Strategy Pattern?

- **A)** Reduces memory usage.
- **B)** Reduces the number of classes in the system.
- **C)** Reduces if-else and switch statements.
- **D)** Increases code complexity.

Answer: C) Reduces if-else and switch statements.

Question 8

Which design pattern is most similar to the Strategy Pattern?

- **A)** Singleton Pattern
- **B)** State Pattern
- **C)** Observer Pattern
- **D)** Prototype Pattern

Answer: B) State Pattern

Question 9

Which of the following best describes the Strategy Pattern?

- **A)** It allows for dynamic method dispatch at runtime.
- **B)** It defines a family of algorithms and makes them interchangeable at runtime.
- **C)** It enforces a single responsibility principle.
- **D)** It creates an abstract factory of methods.

Answer: B) It defines a family of algorithms and makes them interchangeable at runtime.

Question 10

Which of the following is NOT a component of the Strategy Pattern?

- **A)** Context
- **B)** Strategy
- **C)** Singleton
- **D)** Concrete Strategy

Answer: C) Singleton

Question 11

How can you change the behavior of an object at runtime using the Strategy Pattern?

- **A)** Use `Object.assign()`
- **B)** Change the strategy in the context
- **C)** Use `this.bind()`
- **D)** Modify the prototype of the context

Answer: B) Change the strategy in the context

Question 12

What is the purpose of the **Context** in the Strategy Pattern?

- **A)** To select which strategy to use at runtime.
- **B)** To act as a central point for object creation.
- **C)** To provide a common interface for all strategies.
- **D)** To prevent the use of switch statements.

Answer: A) To select which strategy to use at runtime.

Coding Exercises with Solutions

Exercise 1: Calculator Strategy

Task: Implement a `Calculator` class that can perform addition, subtraction, multiplication, and division.
Solution:

```
const add = {
  calculate: (a, b) => a + b
};
```

```javascript
const subtract = {
  calculate: (a, b) => a - b
};


const multiply = {
  calculate: (a, b) => a * b
};


const divide = {
  calculate: (a, b) => a / b
};


function Calculator(strategy) {
  this.strategy = strategy;
}


Calculator.prototype.setStrategy =
function(strategy) {
```

```javascript
    this.strategy = strategy;
};


Calculator.prototype.calculate = function(a, b)
{
    return this.strategy.calculate(a, b);
};


const calculator = new Calculator(add);
console.log(calculator.calculate(10, 5)); //
Output: 15


calculator.setStrategy(multiply);
console.log(calculator.calculate(10, 5)); //
Output: 50
```

Exercise 2: Sorting Strategy

Task: Implement sorting strategies for BubbleSort, MergeSort, and QuickSort.

182

Solution:

```
const bubbleSort = {
  sort: (arr) => arr.sort((a, b) => a - b)
};


const reverseSort = {
  sort: (arr) => arr.sort((a, b) => b - a)
};


function Sorter(strategy) {
  this.strategy = strategy;
}


Sorter.prototype.setStrategy =
function(strategy) {
  this.strategy = strategy;
};
```

```javascript
Sorter.prototype.sort = function(arr) {
  return this.strategy.sort(arr);
};


const sorter = new Sorter(bubbleSort);
console.log(sorter.sort([4, 2, 5, 1])); //
Output: [1, 2, 4, 5]


sorter.setStrategy(reverseSort);
console.log(sorter.sort([4, 2, 5, 1])); //
Output: [5, 4, 2, 1]
```

Exercise 3: Game Character Strategy

Task: Implement strategies for attacking, defending, and healing.
Solution:

```javascript
const attack = {
```

```
  action: () => console.log('Attacking the
enemy!')
};


const defend = {
  action: () => console.log('Defending against
the attack!')
};


const heal = {
  action: () => console.log('Healing up!')
};


function Character(strategy) {
  this.strategy = strategy;
}


Character.prototype.setStrategy =
function(strategy) {
```

```
    this.strategy = strategy;
};


Character.prototype.action = function() {
    this.strategy.action();
};


const character = new Character(attack);
character.action(); // Output: Attacking the
enemy!
```

Exercise 4: Payment Strategy

Create a PaymentContext where users can switch between
Credit Card, PayPal, and Crypto payments.
Solution:

```
const CreditCard = { pay: amount =>
console.log(`Paid $${amount} with Credit Card`)
};
```

```
const PayPal = { pay: amount =>
console.log(`Paid $${amount} with PayPal`) };
const Crypto = { pay: amount =>
console.log(`Paid $${amount} with
Cryptocurrency`) };


function PaymentContext(strategy) {
  this.strategy = strategy;
}


PaymentContext.prototype.setStrategy =
function(strategy) {
  this.strategy = strategy;
};


PaymentContext.prototype.pay = function(amount)
{
  this.strategy.pay(amount);
};
```

```
const payment = new PaymentContext(CreditCard);
payment.pay(100); // Paid $100 with Credit Card


payment.setStrategy(PayPal);
payment.pay(50); // Paid $50 with PayPal
```

Exercise 5: Notification Strategy

Task:

Create a notification system that can send notifications via **SMS**, **Email**, or **Push Notification**.

Solution:

```
// Define strategy objects
const smsNotification = { notify: (message) =>
console.log(`SMS: ${message}`) };
const emailNotification = { notify: (message)
=> console.log(`Email: ${message}`) };
const pushNotification = { notify: (message) =>
console.log(`Push Notification: ${message}`) };
```

```javascript
// Context
function NotificationContext(strategy) {
  this.strategy = strategy;
}


NotificationContext.prototype.setStrategy =
function(strategy) {
  this.strategy = strategy;
};


NotificationContext.prototype.send =
function(message) {
  this.strategy.notify(message);
};


// Usage
const notification = new
NotificationContext(smsNotification);
notification.send('Hello!'); // SMS: Hello!
```

```
notification.setStrategy(emailNotification);
notification.send('Check your inbox.'); //
Email: Check your inbox.
```

```
notification.setStrategy(pushNotification);
notification.send('New alert!'); // Push
Notification: New alert!
```

Explanation:
- The `NotificationContext` allows switching between different notification types at runtime.
- The `send()` method sends the message according to the selected strategy.

Exercise 6: Shipping Strategy

Task:
A shipping company wants to calculate shipping costs based on **Ground**, **Air**, and **Sea** strategies. Implement a `ShippingContext` that allows switching between these strategies.

Solution:

```
// Define strategy objects
const groundShipping = { calculate: (weight) =>
weight * 1.5 };
const airShipping = { calculate: (weight) =>
weight * 3 };
const seaShipping = { calculate: (weight) =>
weight * 0.8 };


// Context
function ShippingContext(strategy) {
  this.strategy = strategy;
}


ShippingContext.prototype.setStrategy =
function(strategy) {
  this.strategy = strategy;
};
```

```
ShippingContext.prototype.calculateCost =
function(weight) {
  return this.strategy.calculate(weight);
};


// Usage
const shipping = new
ShippingContext(groundShipping);
console.log(shipping.calculateCost(10)); //
Cost for ground shipping


shipping.setStrategy(airShipping);
console.log(shipping.calculateCost(10)); //
Cost for air shipping


shipping.setStrategy(seaShipping);
console.log(shipping.calculateCost(10)); //
Cost for sea shipping
```

Explanation:

- The ShippingContext allows the user to calculate shipping costs using different methods.

Exercise 7: Compression Strategy

Task:
Compress files using different algorithms: **Zip**, **Rar**, and **7zip**.
Solution:

```
const zipCompression = { compress: (file) =>
console.log(`Compressing ${file} using Zip`) };
const rarCompression = { compress: (file) =>
console.log(`Compressing ${file} using Rar`) };
const sevenZipCompression = { compress: (file)
=> console.log(`Compressing ${file} using
7zip`) };


function CompressionContext(strategy) {
  this.strategy = strategy;
}
```

```javascript
CompressionContext.prototype.setStrategy =
function(strategy) {
  this.strategy = strategy;
};


CompressionContext.prototype.compressFile =
function(file) {
  this.strategy.compress(file);
};


// Usage
const compression = new
CompressionContext(zipCompression);
compression.compressFile('file.txt'); //
Compressing file.txt using Zip


compression.setStrategy(rarCompression);
compression.compressFile('file.txt'); //
Compressing file.txt using Rar
```

```
compression.setStrategy(sevenZipCompression);
compression.compressFile('file.txt'); //
Compressing file.txt using 7zip
```

Explanation:

- The CompressionContext allows files to be compressed using different strategies.

Exercise 8: Logging Strategy

Task:
Switch between logging messages to the **console**, **file**, or **API** endpoint.
Solution:

```
const consoleLogger = { log: (message) =>
console.log(`Console Log: ${message}`) };
const fileLogger = { log: (message) =>
console.log(`Logging to file: ${message}`) };
```

```javascript
const apiLogger = { log: (message) =>
console.log(`Sending log to API: ${message}`)
};


function LoggerContext(strategy) {
  this.strategy = strategy;
}


LoggerContext.prototype.setStrategy =
function(strategy) {
  this.strategy = strategy;
};


LoggerContext.prototype.log = function(message)
{
  this.strategy.log(message);
};


// Usage
```

```
const logger = new
LoggerContext(consoleLogger);
logger.log('User logged in'); // Console Log:
User logged in


logger.setStrategy(fileLogger);
logger.log('User performed an action'); //
Logging to file: User performed an action


logger.setStrategy(apiLogger);
logger.log('User logged out'); // Sending log
to API: User logged out
```

Exercise 9: Encryption Strategy

Task:
Encrypt a message using **AES**, **RSA**, and **Base64** encryption algorithms.
Solution:

```javascript
const aesEncryption = { encrypt: (data) =>
`AES(${data})` };
const rsaEncryption = { encrypt: (data) =>
`RSA(${data})` };
const base64Encryption = { encrypt: (data) =>
btoa(data) };


function EncryptionContext(strategy) {
  this.strategy = strategy;
}


EncryptionContext.prototype.setStrategy =
function(strategy) {
  this.strategy = strategy;
};


EncryptionContext.prototype.encrypt =
function(data) {
  return this.strategy.encrypt(data);
};
```

```javascript
// Usage
const encryption = new
EncryptionContext(aesEncryption);
console.log(encryption.encrypt('myPassword'));
// AES(myPassword)


encryption.setStrategy(rsaEncryption);
console.log(encryption.encrypt('myPassword'));
// RSA(myPassword)


encryption.setStrategy(base64Encryption);
console.log(encryption.encrypt('myPassword'));
// Base64 encoded version
```

Conclusion

Congratulations on completing the **JavaScript Handbook: Design Patterns**. By mastering these fundamental patterns, you have taken a significant step toward becoming a **confident, efficient, and versatile developer**. From **Module and**

Singleton to **Factory and Observer**, you've explored the tools that top developers use daily to create maintainable, scalable applications.

But this is just the beginning. Design patterns are the **cornerstone of modern software development**, and your journey to mastery continues as you encounter new problems and discover creative ways to apply these patterns. Keep exploring, keep experimenting, and most importantly, keep coding.

This book is part of a broader **JavaScript Handbook series** aimed at providing in-depth, practical learning experiences. As you grow your skills, look out for the next books in the series, covering advanced JavaScript topics like **Functional Programming, Advanced Functions, and Asynchronous Programming**.

Your next step? Start applying what you've learned in your own projects. The more you practice, the more natural these patterns will become. Write, debug, and refactor your code, and remember that even seasoned developers revisit design patterns to sharpen their skills. You now have the knowledge and tools to take on larger, more complex projects with confidence.

About the Author

Laurence Lars Svekis is a renowned web developer, best-selling author, and sought-after educator with over two decades of experience in JavaScript and modern web development. As a **Google Developer Expert (GDE)**, he is celebrated for his work with **Google Apps Script** and his expertise in **JavaScript, functional programming, and asynchronous development**. With over **one million students worldwide**, Laurence's interactive courses, live presentations, and books have empowered developers of all levels. His clear, hands-on approach makes complex concepts accessible, from closures to async programming and beyond. A prolific author and active contributor to the developer community, Laurence's work inspires developers to master JavaScript, build scalable applications, and achieve success in the fast-evolving world of software development.

Explore his resources and learn more at **BaseScripts.com**.

www.ingramcontent.com/pod-product-compliance
Lightning Source LLC
LaVergne TN
LVHW051230050326
832903LV00028B/2332